A Single Mother's Memoir of Self-Love,
Empowerment and Freedom

WHO
WILL
HOLD
ME?

Sophie Pagalday

WHO WILL HOLD ME?
A Single Mothers' Memoir of Self-Love, Empowerment and Freedom

Copyright © 2019 by Sophie Pagalday

ISBN-13: 978-0-578-59510-8

www.sophiepagalday.com

Dedication

To my Spiritual Master, whom I still rebel against. (She doesn't mind.) Thank you for showing me a path with more joy than I ever knew possible.

To my daughter, who has been the most loving and bravest companion on this journey. Never try to take two strong-willed girls down. We'll show you what we're made of.

To my partner, who loves me like I didn't know humans could love. My best friend, who tells the worst jokes at the most inappropriate times. I really, really need those jokes. Thank you for preventing me from taking myself too seriously.

To everyone who has served as my teacher and guide, I'm forever grateful for the times we've held each other in our pain and imperfections with unconditional love and compassion. You know who you are.

"Do you want to be a writer, and speak to others and for others? Speak first for yourself. Search within. Consider the contents of your own soul. Your humanity. And if you're honest with yourself, then whatever you write, all is true."

—Branagh, K. (Director), & Berwick, L. (Executive Producer) (2018). *All Is True* [Motion Picture]. United States: TKBC.

BECAUSE EVERY SINGLE MOTHER HAS A STORY...

I'd love to hear yours.

THE AWAKENING SINGLE MOM

is a community where single mothers can get up-close and personal with the material from the book "Who Will Hold Me? A Single Mother's Memoir of Self-Love, Empowerment & Freedom." It's a drama-free, blame-free space for all single moms embarking on their own journey of self-discovery and seeking support in a shared experience.

Members can enjoy the inside track on specific tools and practices that have helped Sophie and join her on weekly calls answering questions and sharing experiences.

It's also a place where other single moms who are on a similar path can connect with one another and share their own tips and gems they've picked up along the way.

JOIN THE COMMUNITY BY SCANNING THE QR CODE

Introduction

While others may have seen the writing on the wall, I had to take a serious look within to realize I needed a divorce. I've always been a fixer, and a good one at that. But it wasn't until I embarked on a deep journey of self-discovery that it finally dawned on me that I wasn't living the life I wanted. Somewhere along the path, I had gotten so far removed from my true nature that I could barely recognize myself anymore.

I started looking for something that would bring me back to life and reconnect me with my passion. The deeper I went into myself and the closer I got to what I've always wanted, the clearer it became that my marriage of seven years no longer fit.

Making the decision to get divorced almost immediately granted me the title of single mother. Alone, heartbroken, and confused, I committed myself to making sense of the snowball of chaos that had become my life, which included watching my ex-husband's addiction set him on his own journey of pain and self-destruction. My new reality involved fully taking care of my then three-year-old daughter emotionally and financially—and in every other way possible.

This all happened in the midst of my spiritual awakening, if I may humbly call it that. At times, it has been hard to see the light at the end of the tunnel. In between, I've been blessed with a spiritual practice that has helped me let go of what had been holding me back all along. I've found new ways to be calm in the middle of the storm and to fall in love with my path, even though it's not always been an easy journey.

Along the way, I have learned invaluable lessons that guide me to this day. And, it wouldn't be fair to speak of these learnings without acknowledging the mistakes and darkness I've had to face within myself to get to this place. With this book, my commitment is to be open and vulnerable to share all of it with you.

This is my story to the best of my recollection, and I humbly recognize that we can each see only as far as our awareness will allow us at any given moment. I do my best to respect everyone's privacy while also sharing important events related to the unfolding of my inner journey.

I will mention my Spiritual Master throughout the book. I will not share her name out of respect for her and her disciples, as well as to prevent them from having to manage any unwanted media attention. Each of them is on a sacred and personal spiritual path, as am I.

To appreciate and learn from my story, you don't have to subscribe to any belief system or way of thinking. If nothing else, my hope is that sharing my story will allow you to embrace your own perspective and all that comes with it.

In the end, I'm sharing my journey to convey a simple message. You can choose your way out of the chaos and the drama. You don't have to deny your very real pain. You have the power within yourself to overcome the hard times without struggle. You have the power to build an abundant life. You have the heart to hold space for your children and yourself.

I know. This may sound too good to be true. You have your children's homework, dinner, and bills to worry about. Then, you need to do the dishes and get that presentation ready for tomorrow. You go to sleep crying (when you're not collapsing on the couch after the kids have fallen asleep). I'm human and have experienced nights like this more than I'd like to admit. But if you can find a moment to let me take you on this journey, you may just not feel so alone.

Chapter One

AS I WAIT TO board the plane, I feel my phone vibrate in my back pocket. The caller ID displays "Unknown." I immediately dismiss the call as spam and send it straight to voicemail. When a second call from Unknown reaches me, my chest tightens as a feeling of uncertainty creeps up from my stomach, up my spine and into my head. I'm dizzy. As I decide whether I should answer, I search my mind for any bad news I should be expecting. There's nothing. Why am I so hesitant to pick up?

Although I've never spoken to this particular police officer before, what he reports isn't completely foreign. Sean, my ex-husband, has been arrested again, and I need to pick up my seven-year-old daughter, Zoey, from a random gas station.

Taking a few deep breaths to help me stay focused and think clearly, I ask, "Is she okay?" as if I could somehow assess the wounds in her heart by having the officer take a quick look at her. I'm relieved to hear she isn't physically hurt, but having fought the shadows of my own trauma before, I know what it's like to innocently face the world when it finally shows you what it's made of.

I don't panic, but I feel consumed by my own fear of abandonment. It's really disturbing how, even when we legitimately care about what another is going through, our worries are born of and filtered through our own deepest fears. Would her young mind take this memory and build a strong case for how, no matter how great things seem for a while, she will eventually be abandoned again? We project such fears onto the ones we're concerned about rather than holding space for them to identify their own pain and needs.

I couldn't get to Zoey fast enough, but my partner, Ben, could. Although Ben isn't Zoey's father, he's very organically taken a paternal role in her life. He doesn't have children of his own, but his big heart cares so deeply. Since he appeared in our lives over a year ago, he's loved Zoey and me in ways we didn't know were possible.

Breathing deeply to prevent my fear from taking over, I call Ben and briefly explain what has happened.

"Of course, I can pick her up," he reassures me. "Where is she? Get on the plane. We'll be okay."

After giving him my daughter's exact coordinates, I need to think for a moment. What will Zoey need tonight and in the next few days? Yes, Ben will take care of her while I'm away on my business trip, but it isn't just about that. I fear that seeing her dad being arrested will bring up new feelings and leave her confused. The only thing to do is to turn around and be there for her.

I call a colleague and text my boss. I don't know how to explain what has happened, so I creatively modify the story to make it a little more digestible.

"My ex-husband and daughter have been in a car accident. I need to make sure she's okay. I won't be able to make the flight."

My preferred approach of being brutally honest is rarely well received. I go back and forth, believing that sugarcoating is a way of denial while sometimes wavering and spoon-feeding others only what they're ready to hear. I've also experienced the stigma of being a single mother with a complicated situation. Almost every time, sharing the truth has led to assumptions about what I can handle at work and whether I'm capable of taking on a promotion. Not to mention, "my ex-husband has been arrested again" is not necessarily watercooler conversation.

As I walk back to the terminal, I get another call from the same police officer, who offers more details now that Zoey isn't present. A taxi driver who drove Sean to Zoey's summer camp reported him. The driver didn't feel my daughter was safe with Sean in his current intoxicated state. She dropped them both off at a gas station on the way back to his house and called the police.

I am not surprised at any of this, not just because this isn't my first rodeo, but also because Sean had told me he had broken his probation a few days ago.

"I'll probably go back to jail and get raped or in a fight. But, Zoey has it a lot worse outside of jail with all the mass shootings lately," Sean had reflected on his outlook.

Should I have known better when he told me that he'd have lots of notice on his new court date? Like a fool falling for the same old trick, I trusted everything would turn out okay this time. Perhaps that anxiety when the phone rang was guilt creeping up again? How many more times will I allow him to put our daughter at risk? How has this become part of our casual phone conversations?

All of this terrifies me. No matter how dark the world is, the choice of bringing a new sentence upon himself by violating his court order is something I can't reconcile.

At her young age, Zoey has already experienced the loss of a loved one multiple times. She has said goodbye to her dad, even if temporarily, every time he's relapsed, neglected her, put himself back into an inpatient rehab program, or gone to jail. Zoey's paternal grandmother, her most positive connection to her dad, passed away a year ago. And she recently lost her hamster. How much more can her young heart take? Is it appropriate for a seven-year-old to be this familiar with the stages of grief?

As for Sean, he's not the kind of guy who's cut out for jail. At five foot ten, he barely weighs twice as much as my daughter. A former philosophy major, he looks more like he belongs in front of a class at a university than in a cell. Sometimes, I have a hard time understanding how he went from being the man who had traveled the world looking for answers to the deepest questions, to struggling to create a fulfilling life. Then again, if there's one thing I've learned, it's that serious seekers are deeply connected to the pain of the world. The answers to many of the questions we all wonder about at some point or another are very hard to digest, especially without guidance from something greater than ourselves.

In any case, I thought we were past the phase of daily chaos, drama, and trauma. Sean has been out of jail for about a year and has been regaining a place in Zoey's life. He has once again proven that he can be a good dad when he's sober.

Why lose it all again?

My phone rings again, and this time it is my daughter calling from Ben's car. She is surprisingly cheerful. She explains that the taxi driver just took off, and that she and her dad sat on the sidewalk until the police came. They were allowed to say goodbye, and she cried as he was driven away.

"The police officers were very nice and let me sit in the front seat of their car. I got to spot differences between a police car and your car, Mom. It was fun!"

I don't want to open Pandora's box until I am there to hold her, so I play along while my heart crumbles. Is this really all she's thinking?

When I arrive home, I sit down with Zoey. I want to talk to her and give her a chance to tell me how she is *really* feeling. I encourage her to ask any and all questions she may have about what just happened. She instead tells me the story one more time like it is someone else's life in some movie. I don't hear any feelings in her voice, and she doesn't ask to be comforted. Underestimating both our connection and the space I've always held for her, I repeat more times than necessary that I am here for her and that I can only imagine how she feels. She looks at me and says with determination, "Mom, my body doesn't have any feelings. Please don't force me."

The next morning, I can barely tolerate the heartache and there's only one thing for me to do: light a candle next to a picture of my Spiritual Master, sit on my bedroom floor across from my altar, and collapse into my pain.

On my knees, face between my hands, I sob so deeply that

my core shakes. The more I surrender into my pain, the more I feel the longing to be held. I search for a thread I can tug to unravel my thoughts and feelings, knowing only then can I pull myself back together. It's taken years to be comfortable enough to let myself fall apart, trusting that releasing it all will leave me with more compassion, love, and clarity in the end.

"God, please, please, please guide me one more time through the pain and back into the light." This is a somewhat new practice for me. Only a few years ago, I would have never been able to say the word God out loud. I wouldn't have asked for help or surrendered to my reality.

I was raised with the religious belief that if I didn't behave this or that way, I'd be in serious trouble. Rather than ask for help, I'd better be ready to ask for forgiveness. I should never start by asking, but by reflecting on how undeserving I was. The white-bearded man would point His finger down at me and punish me in oh so many ways.

Today, this word "God" has a very different meaning for me, and it's not one I've been brainwashed into. I don't mean a supreme being sitting on a cloud, controlling the universe and our destiny. You could very well replace the word "God" with Higher Self, Universe, Spirit, Source, or the Divine. It's not mine to decide how you relate to that power, the energy of love and light. What's undeniable for me is that I've very personally found a connection with Him within, buried underneath all of my pain and helplessness. Miraculously, perhaps, this didn't happen while searching for a belief system I could subscribe to, but during my unavoidable internal fight for Truth. He's held me at times when no one else was there to hold me. And I mean *really* hold me, like no human ever has.

6

Personifying God makes it easier to share my experience with this force of love and light. But that's not the only reason I refer to the Divine as "He" and "Him." Besides attempting to give this powerful energy the respect He deserves, I also have an intimate relationship with Him. He's responded to my prayers and desires, so He must be able to hear me. He's shown me the way by helping me open my heart and painting my canvas with new opportunities, so He must have will. When I trust, He works through me in miraculous ways so I can discover what I've been looking for all along.

The choice of "He" versus "She" is likely in part about some lingering conditioning— likely mirroring the relationship with my mother and my father, and how I was taught to pray. But there's a part that's very mine and has to do with how I relate to Him. In my up-and-close experiences, the energy has felt paternal and protective.

Back to my bedroom floor. Crawled into a ball, I try to somehow reconcile what is happening in my heart and how each of us—Zoey, Sean, Ben, and I—have been impacted by the recent events.

Zoey adores her dad and longs for his love. Even though she's learned about loss too early in her life, her young heart is braver than most. I pray that she fights the human instinct to attach her self-worth onto how fairly life has treated her so far.

Sean is still in search of a way out of his own suffering. How can I blame him when I understand addiction is a force of darkness that will drag the purest hearts into complete hell? I pray that he finds the strength to crawl his way out of the hole he's dug for himself.

Ben looks for justice and a way to protect Zoey and me. He now has a family he wants to see thrive. I pray that he finds compassion for all of us, including Sean.

There is nothing to work through in my mind. So much is out of my hands. Blaming will only perpetuate the pain. Perpetuating the pain will take us back into struggle. I just have to do my part.

The next couple of days, my feelings are all over the place, as if caught in a blender turning chunks of pain into something that can nurture my heart. Each of us wants things to be different, but rather than fight reality, we attempt to cope. My daughter is clingy. My partner is angry. My ex-husband sounds terrified as he begs me to bail him out. I sob every chance I get.

Even in the midst of all this crying, something is different for me. For the first time in my life, I decline the invitation to my own pity party. These tears are not born of helplessness and defeat. So many times, I have gone into that victim place where all I can feel is anger, desperation, and resentment. But this time, I feel I have forgiven my ex-husband, myself, how unfair this world can be, and the fact that we're all driven by our own pain.

This time, I trust everything is going to be okay. I'm going to be okay. My daughter is going to be okay. Ben is going to be okay. Sean is going to be okay. I can feel I have let go of expectations, of wanting things my way, of wanting to control my own and everyone else's suffering. I'm not resigned. Instead, I trust. I trust my ability to build a life that supports us in getting through the next thing, and the next thing, and the next thing. Because I've done it. Every time. Each time, with less drama, clutter, mess, and chaos than the previous time.

But before I get too cocky on my bedroom floor about all

my awareness only hours after another traumatic scene, let me take you back to the beginning.

I still remember when things weren't this way. In our small town in the foothills of the Rocky Mountain range, there's one mountain I always climb when I need to come up for air.

The first time I went to this mountain, all I could see were sleepy brown bushes and thirsty dirt. But on a recent visit on a sunny afternoon, the hills and valleys were bright green, and I could see my beautiful home down below. Standing up there, I knew that every trip up and down the mountain represented me going through one more layer of my pain and getting closer to my freedom.

When I look back now, I don't ask myself why I married Sean; why I gave Zoey this father, or who will hold me. Over and over again, I have been shown that what's happening right now is exactly what needs to happen. It's just that I haven't yet had the patience or the willingness to endure the pain to see what's on the other side. I'm now familiar with the inherent trap of shortcuts, and how sticking with the path in front of me instead has enabled my heart to open up to more love than I imagined possible. Every time I've embraced my reality rather than looked for the quickest exit into pleasure, a new part of my soul has been uncovered. From this place, things just flow.

Holding myself—that ability to cradle my own heart with gentleness and compassion when things are falling apart—is not just this magical thing I've learned overnight. I'm not miraculously enlightened and know everything I need to know. I don't always succeed either. This feeling of fulfillment, peace, and freedom doesn't come from success and wealth or achieving some sense of material security. The pieces of the puzzle are scattered and hidden in the most unexpected places. Every time I'm willing to face the next hurdle with a positive attitude, my eyes open wide and I can see the next piece. Most times, the puzzle piece was right there all along, I was just blinded by my own suffering.

Chapter Two

STANDING IN THE HALLWAY of our beautiful home in the suburbs, I feel a tiny hand pull on my dress. With tears in my eyes, I look down at my three-year-old daughter to take a brief break from my husband's angry stare. The voice of the youngest human, yet oldest soul in my life, reminds me of a truth I had recently discovered. "It's not okay for him to talk to you that way, Mommy. I think we should go."

If I were in a movie, this would have been one of those scenes where the soundtrack gives you a clue this is a defining moment in a character's life. I had just come back from a meditation retreat that had slowed my whole world down. Over the last four days, I bravely walked into every dark corner of my existence to stand face-to-face with the dark truths I had avoided for so long.

From a detached distance, I feel many complex emotions flowing through my heart and looking for the exit tunnel into the light. My mouth doesn't run to respond to make things right, for a change. My mind searches for answers in the depths of my heart, rather than along the familiar, warn paths carved into my mind.

In a few seconds, I journey deep into my soul and back, and it becomes clear I have two options: I either flat out lie to my daughter, reassuring her that everything is just fine and thereby demonstrating that this is an okay way to be treated; or I let her see me walk through the fire, holding courage in one hand and fear in the other. Full of conviction that the truth is worth every burn, I say, "You're right, baby. Let's go."

As I turn toward the staircase, my husband's slim shadow stumbles into the kitchen. Relieved to have avoided further interaction, I climb each step slowly, as if the weight of my heart is too heavy to carry up the stairs. I feel determined and in complete disbelief that I'm finally, really doing it. I'm taking the step I've long dreaded: putting an end to my marriage, or rather, finally letting it fall apart. Where will Zoey and I go? I tell myself I can't make the next twenty decisions now, so I pray and pack.

My daughter is waiting for me at the bottom of the stairs. She seems as determined as I am. I pick her up, grab our bags, and head out to the garage, wondering whether her father will follow or try to stop us. As I buckle my daughter up in the back seat, my heart pounds. I don't doubt myself for one moment, but I cannot ignore the fear running through my veins. Can I simply walk away from the life I have built and create a new one out of nothing?

I drive aimlessly around our neighborhood as I plan my next move. I've done a wonderful job of hiding my husband's addiction, and my misery, until this weekend, so my options feel limited. One of the few people I can call is my friend Stella, who's been like a sister to me. Since she's a fellow Latin American, I know it's never too late or too intrusive to ask if we can crash on her couch. Her house is small, but her generous heart and selfless intentions somehow always seem to create extra space to welcome those who need shelter.

As we drive toward the mountains to Stella, my daughter points out in her usual poetic way, that the moon is following us.

"I think she wants to make sure we're safe, Mommy," she says confidently.

We both need to hear that we are safe. A few clouds cover the moon along the way, and Zoey points out that the moon is playing hide and seek with us to make us smile. We both need to know we'll smile again. Falling apart on the inside, I naturally engage in this game because, besides each other, that's all we have in that moment.

When we arrive at Stella's house, all we're greeted with is a comforting, "Are you okay?" We all go right to sleep. We will talk in the morning.

⚜

I wish I'd always been this clear about what I want; this determined to stand for what I deserve. Or perhaps I have been those things, even if I couldn't recognize it until now. Not long ago, an unexpected yet very real impulse from within propelled me to connect with myself. Somewhere along the way, I had abandoned the free little girl who wanted to be a hummingbird so she'd never have to live in a cage. But I had tricked myself into willingly building my own enclosure, even believing that the "safety" of captivity was what I longed for. Now that thought alone makes me feel claustrophobic and want to jump out of my own skin.

Four days ago, I didn't have this awareness or any idea of how to untangle myself out of the trap I felt I was in. For longer than I'd like to admit, I had subconsciously put myself in situations that validated that I was not worthy of love and should simply get used to rejection. When I eventually found someone who was willing to marry me, I took that opportunity. Completely oblivious that a part of me was only seeking a quick fix to some deeper wound, I sealed the deal and dove into marriage as if that was validation enough.

I'm not saying that's the only reason I married Sean. Our relationship did start out with plenty of adventures. But, once we ran out of fun things to do, we bought into the rat race. We began by acquiring what we were taught we needed to have: the beautiful house in the suburbs with brand new furniture and a lifestyle that required us to work harder and harder every day. As we went through the motions, this routine took a toll on both of us, but we just kept putting one foot in front of the other, never truly having a heart-to-heart conversation about how dissatisfied we were. Where had the hopeful, fun travelers gone?

Next thing we knew, it was time to have children. While this decision was in part born of an altruistic desire to create something together, what followed was a trying year of disappointment when the conversation we had been avoiding became a potential reason we weren't getting pregnant. I started blaming our bad luck on his addiction and obsessed over potential solutions. On our way back from another anniversary dinner, just after I had built a case that we needed professional help, I found myself with a positive pregnancy test in my hand.

As I delivered the news, his terrified face was the exact same one he wore on the day we got married. First, I panicked. Had we made another mistake? Then, taken over by my own excitement, I locked all my anxiety about our marriage and being pregnant in a safe corner of my heart. We could now officially pretend everything was fine.

Over the next nine months, things got worse between us. I truly wanted to be happy about being pregnant, but the truth is, I was terrified. No matter how many positive affirmations I shoved into my brain about how he would fall in love with being a parent and simply quit drinking, that felt farther from our destiny with every sunset. He found comfort in his drinking, and I found it in food. I easily gained fifty pounds. With every bite, I swallowed chunks of rejection, neglect, and fear of raising our daughter around my husband.

Between five and six o'clock every evening, he'd pull the tab on his first can of beer, letting the dreaded hissing sound echo in the kitchen. I'd sigh and feel defeated one more time. I was reminded that I couldn't win that battle. In fact, I had no business fighting that battle.

Then there were those nights when I felt I had to make myself heard, no matter how many times I had already proven it was a waste of my time. I'd ruminate on how neglected I felt and how this was the last family that needed a baby. How would he help me with our daughter as he stumbled his way around the house? Who would help me change diapers or feed the baby in the middle of the night after he had once again passed out on the couch? Why couldn't he just get sober and be present for the people he loved?

Every time, my futile attempt was met with the same infuriating response.

"I drink because of you, because you drive me crazy. I didn't want any of this in the first place."

Had I actually created all of this on my own? Had I subconsciously steered us toward building this life? To this day, I still believe we both created that world. Yet, I also now know we both had a choice about what came next.

Zoey was born in the middle of a warm night in May. While I don't remember much, I do know my husband was by my side for the eight hours I was in labor. He also cheered me along as I gave birth to our beautiful daughter. To this day, I'm grateful that the first thing she ever saw was both our faces in complete awe and love. Zoey's first picture is of her wrapped in her dad's arms, his eyes tearing up and his smile wider than most pictures anyone has ever seen of him.

I've never doubted his love for her. Just like with me, his addiction was the only thing that would ever put her second. And he wasn't even choosing it. Even today, I know that's the truth. Being immersed in that reality and feeling second to a disease is likely the reason that, even with all the love in his heart, my daughter's first month in the world was the hardest one of my life.

Although never officially diagnosed, I'm pretty sure I had post-partum depression. Being so vulnerable after giving birth, it seemed impossible to overwrite what felt like a biological need to be protected and loved. I was physically healing, my hormones were unstable, and I was incredibly sleep deprived. I felt fat, tired, and cranky beyond measure, which didn't necessarily help my self-esteem. On the other hand, my husband seemed to be in complete shock and unable to meet my expectations of love and support. If I hadn't had my mother to take the baby off my hands and encourage me to take a moment to shower and feel "normal" again, I probably would have lost it.

In my depressed state, I continued to hope things would change and that someday his own paternal instinct would kick in. Even with all evidence pointing to the opposite, I kept trying to be the wife and mother I felt I needed to be. I kept wishing he'd join my daughter and me as we adopted evening adventures along the nearby trails. I cooked dinner every night, hoping he wouldn't just sniff the food and tell me he wasn't "going to eat that crap."

Then one day, Mars was twenty-six degrees from Libra and above Venus, according to my natal chart, which launched me into a series of decisions that would eventually change everything. I had just—somewhat randomly, I thought—decided to try a yoga class because I needed to find some kind of physical and mental balance. Yoga classes led to meditation sessions at the studio, which led my friend Lucia to introduce me to her practice and the woman who would become my Spiritual Master.

Lucia and I had been co-workers and then friends for a handful of years. She'd followed this Spiritual Master for over a decade, yet I'd never heard her mention meditation or her spiritual path until she offered to guide a meditation just for me, in the privacy of my home. If it hadn't been for previous yoga classes or that religion teacher in Catholic school who opened our eyes to how every tradition (in the end) shows us a different path to the same ultimate goal, I might not have taken Lucia up on the offer to join her Wednesday community meditations.

On the evening of that first Wednesday meditation, I nervously walked into the old, converted church. It wasn't just the traditional stained-glass windows or the floor-to-ceiling altar displaying deities and masters from multiple religions and lineages that gave the meditation room its sacred feeling. There was—and there still is—something intangible, an energy that carried me as I entered the building that's now been my sanctuary for years.

It didn't take long for me to find a spot in the meditation room where I could admire the entire altar. First, I was drawn to a painting depicting 'Light Beings.' There has always been something familiar about these tall, white figures wrapped in glowing robes. I could feel my soul among them, protecting us all.

Eventually, I dared to look to the right of this painting at a photo of the Spiritual Master and founder of the practice. Even from a distance, it was apparent her piercing eyes were watchful and could see right through my mask. She could look beyond appearances, even the personality I carefully crafted to protect my heart, and see the burning desire in my soul. This was intimidating, to say the least.

Since hearing her words firsthand, I've experienced a kind of love I never knew existed. She's willing to speak the truth, even when I'm not ready to listen, even when my selective hearing filters things out—even when what she says triggers my deepest fears, false core beliefs, and the need to protect the habits I've developed to cope with the pain of this world. She doesn't care if I like her. Her love for me—for all of us—is so unconditional that she wants nothing but my freedom, whatever it takes. And what it takes, I've learned from her words and my own experience, is to face all those feelings that trip me up... and let them go—to surrender into whatever truth is hiding underneath.

Weekly meditation and a vibrant spiritual practice were just what I needed. I recognized the gift of having guidance from someone with an awareness far beyond mine. I had also been longing for that embrace and a safe space to go when life's hardships became too much to bear. In those moments, my Spiritual Master's watchful stare felt more like that of a protective mama bear.

As the weeks and months passed, this seemingly simple act of going into deep meditation weekly and listening to my Spiritual Master's teachings started to show me a new world within myself. Incrementally letting go of repetitive negative thoughts that led to the same unhealthy actions, I started to uncover and rekindle my lost passion to live a meaningful life and grow through challenges. I wanted more. Without any idea of how this simple act would be pivotal in my life, I told Lucia I wanted to attend the next retreat.

In the first moments of the first day of my first meditation retreat, we were asked to let go of what we thought this experience would be. While uncertainty often results in my entire being becoming possessed by the control-freak in me, this proposition oddly sounded like music to my ears this time. I dove in like there was no other place to be and nothing else to do. I'd waited long enough to "take out the trash," as my Spiritual Master would say.

As I prepared to go into the meditation room, my heart pulled on my mind, showing the noisy upstairs neighbor that there was something I needed to connect to. *Where's my passion? What's all this pain in my heart about?* I pondered as I followed my fellow meditators on a prayer walk.

With every step, my feelings intensified. I felt a presence that I recognized from the hundreds of evening meditations I'd sat in. It felt even more tangible that day and gave me permission to fall apart, to let the darkest secrets out and confront them all. The pit of my stomach felt like a pressure cooker about to explode. Trapped inside was an endless sadness and anger about to spill everywhere. I finally unlocked the lid. It was time.

I was consumed by the deep pain in my heart and started weeping. I felt I might come undone. How could my body even hold that pain?

We were divided into small groups, and our assigned spiritual leaders welcomed us. They would be guiding us through the next few days. I barely knew these people, but there was a sense of trust that created a safe space so we could each travel within wherever we needed to go. Their unconditional love and compassion were evident in their every move, allowing me to open up. As I spoke my first few words of brutally honest truth, I realized I'd been silenced for years. Me—one of the most outspoken people I know! Silenced.

It was such a relief to finally say out loud why I was there, how I'd felt trapped. As I spoke, I felt my heart disconnecting from my mind, which was disconnected from my body, even though they all inhabit the same being. My mind had been making most decisions, trying to fix everything that was broken, and working hard to figure out what the next move should be to create a more perfect happiness.

"We got this!" said my mind, trying to convince my heart

that everything had been, and would be, okay.

"If we do, why do I feel this way?" replied my heart as it raised an eyebrow.

My mind reassured my heart that once we fixed my husband, I would find happiness in my marriage. No doubt, we would turn into the family I'd always wanted. My daughter would finally have the father I'd dreamed of for her. Then, everything would be okay, and I'd feel connected in the flow I'd longed for.

My heart listened patiently and sighed, trying once again to stitch its broken pieces back together.

"What about you, body? What's your part in this?" my heart asked.

My body had simply been going through the motions. When the mind and the heart are fighting for control, all the body can do is obey the latest random instruction.

But I could no longer hide in this internal debate. I was encouraged to share without holding anything back.

What causes me pain? I don't know where to start. Is it the guilt of forcing ourselves to bring a child into this world when I had doubts about whether we could offer a nurturing home? Is it how rejected I've felt as the bottles of vodka and cans of beer have accumulated on the kitchen counter every night? Or the lack of connection when my husband sinks deeper and deeper into himself until he falls asleep on the couch? Is it that he can't remember what we talked about, whether we were intimate, what we shared, or even our arguments the next morning? Is it that I've been pouring myself into my career so I can quantify my worth in dollars and praise? Is it that I've chosen to be lonely by keeping it to myself and putting on a show for the world?

Perhaps it was all of the above. All I wanted was to be held.

We began meditation. Sitting in deep sorrow, I was led into a deeper place in my heart as soon as the music played. Even though there were dozens of us in the room, I felt almost certain the song playing was hand-selected for me. I looked around at the magic of how every person in the retreat was touched by the song in a unique way, as if a fairy waved a wand around the room, waking each of us up with its gentle touch. Miracles were happening, inviting wondrous awakenings tailored to what we each needed. Some of us felt like standing up and dancing. Others cried and screamed.

Augmenting the already deep verses, the spiritual teacher leading the meditation shared words of encouragement as we faced the darkness within. His words provided light like torches as we went deeper inside ourselves. I was touched by the depth of his encouragement. The synchronicity of the guidance and the lyrics made me wonder about the spiritual state of musicians (and all artists, to be fair) when creating. I recognized the spiritual teacher must have felt as I did sometime before, or they wouldn't have been able to show me the way forward. This helped me trust the process.

I could feel the love in how each song was picked as I deeply explored every feeling hiding within me. As I felt the sadness, the anger, the resentment, I peeled away heavy layer after heavy layer, as if removing a blindfold. All I had to do was be willing to feel it all, face those feelings, and let them go—layer after layer. I was encouraged to keep going toward the ultimate pot of gold, that place where I could find enough freedom, awareness, and perspective to see things differently. My next actions would become clear then, I thought.

The first few layers were full of stories, images, and conversations from my current material reality. I tried to let go of the contents of my mind. Each feeling felt like a hook into a story. The longer each story played in my mind, the more the feeling intensified, and the hook became welded into it. We were guided to continue to go through the pain, rather than wallow and get trapped in the story. As I went deeper within, the story faded away.

Slowly releasing the feeling, I started to gain distance and release the story's grip on me. Eventually, I was left with the purest form of pain—a deeper pain than I'd ever experienced. My Spiritual Master calls this "the longing," an emptiness within that no material thing can fill. It's the cry of the soul; our deepest desire for love; a constant prayer for salvation out of our current material predicament. "Whatever it takes, take this pain away from me," I begged God in that moment.

As I prayed, I felt my body releasing the pain gently. It was no longer time to press forward. I simply needed to be. Something filled my heart, a light. I felt I could fly. I stood up and waved my arms as if they were wings. Love filled my heart, a love I'd never felt before. Everything was okay. I was held, finally.

From this place, there was no wondering any longer about my situation. My ego wasn't fighting. My mind wasn't trying to figure anything out. The truth was so palpable that all I had to do was listen and embrace it. I needed to leave my marriage. My husband needed to walk his path, but I got to choose whether I walked beside him. The loving thing to do for both Zoey and me was to walk in a new direction.

I listened, said yes, and acted as soon as I got home.

❧

I wake up at Stella's house. The mountain air smells like a fresh start. Far from home and the most connected to myself I have felt in years (possibly decades), something propels me from within to trust while my mind attempts to catch up with what's happened. For the first time, I'm timidly dipping my toe in new waters of deep commitment and surrender to the truth I've found within.

Before leaving for the retreat, I had preemptively taken an extra day off work to slowly integrate back into my life. This extra day was meant to provide an opportunity for self-care and to let everything I stirred up inside of me slowly fall into place.

Instead, Zoey and I are away from the place that's been our home since she was born, and I'm wondering where we will sleep the next night. Zoey is happy to miss daycare to play with Stella's daughter, but after four transformational days and a very emotional night, I feel like I've been hit by a truck. I need distance from the world and to contemplate my next move.

A bit disoriented, I walk out of Stella's house to run errands. I move slowly, like an astronaut learning to walk in a new environment without the downward pull of gravity. A multitude of emotions flow through my body like the bubbles in a lava lamp. Every hour or so, a bubble floats all the way to the top and bursts. I, in turn, burst into tears. I don't know if they're happy tears or sad tears. Is this a sadness deeper than I can understand, or am I just letting go of what's left of my pain? I walk a few steps, stop, and let my tears roll down my cheeks.

From the outside, I likely look like a hot mess. On the inside, my body, heart, and soul undergo shifts at a cellular level. That's the best way I can describe how I feel. I'm being rewired from the inside out. Some deep transformation has been set in motion, and all I can do is let it completely unfold.

I barely know what to do with my open, tender heart. For so long, I've kept it blindfolded so that it wouldn't have to endure the pain. I became a workaholic so I wouldn't have to face my life, but with each minute I put into work after hours, I denied myself what I wanted. All of a sudden, I'm catching up on years of being paralyzed and trapped in a reality I would have never consciously chosen. I don't want to even think about going back to work tomorrow. I just want to live my life.

Each interaction with every person I meet goes right through me. I watch my thoughts. I feel the other person. I hear the words being said in the distance, take their essence, let them touch me. I have no defense and no judgement. I could also fall apart again at any second—both from the overwhelming love I feel in my heart and the vulnerability of not knowing how any of this will play out.

This overwhelming love I speak of is not ephemeral. I'm not afraid it will be taken away from me. It's neither attached to a story in my life or mind, nor is it a response to another human being's action or reaction to me. It's just there. I close my eyes, breathe deeply into my chest, and physically feel something has changed. My heart is being held by an invisible, benevolent hand that gently opens and closes with a comforting tightness that is perfectly synchronized with each beat. My heart radiates a loving energy. I can feel it leaving my body and embracing everything and everyone around me.

Although my ego would love to claim otherwise, I recognize this energy is not me or mine. I haven't somehow turned into an enlightened being. This feeling is born of a new connection with God, only possible because, for a moment, I've surrendered to the possibility rather than trying to control my fate. I don't fully understand it or how this happened, but the feeling is undeniable.

I observe myself as I run from errand to errand. Even though I feel like I'm floating, there's a part of me that is still very much human. Even though I have decided to end my marriage, I admit that I'm not ready for what that means. My heart and mind feel slightly at odds.

"The rug has been pulled from under you, and you have to make decisions faster than you're ready for," says my mind.

My always hopeful (and somewhat delirious) mind thought I was going to have some time to decompress, to figure out how to break the news to my husband, negotiate calmly, and jointly decide our next steps. I was naive enough to think that, even though it would be painful for both of us, the transition would be smooth, that I wouldn't have to leave everything but my daughter behind. If I'm being honest, I didn't think Sean would care.

At the retreat, I had been introduced to the concept of duality—the devil and the angel whispering in our ears, the yin and the yang. My Spiritual Master speaks of the manifestation of this duality in our being as an illusory self, or ego; and a true self, otherwise known as the higher self.

Now that I have become somewhat acquainted with this idea of duality, I can feel that, even though I have touched upon some truth, there is still a part of me that, if I became even briefly distracted, might act from fear. I could be ready to pack my bags in one moment, and seriously entertain staying in the familiar, "comfortable" relationship the next.

As I reflect on this internal negotiation, I learn a disturbing truth: the familiar pain of my marriage feels cozier and somehow less painful than the new pain brought on by the thought of "being alone." It's not less painful; it's just that I've become so accustomed to this pain that I've become numb to it. It's how I've protected myself so I can keep going. But it's all pain in the end.

I walk out of the store upon this realization, get in my car, and fall apart. I don't know how to manage this internal battle. Am I being tested to see if I am serious about making change happen? God wouldn't do that to me.

I pick up the phone and call Lucia. She patiently listens to my crying, as usual, but what I have to share isn't about all the suffering in my life. Rather, I ask about how to keep walking in this freedom I've found. I'm confused. She insightfully encourages me to take it one day at a time. I'm reassured that I'm having a normal emotional reaction to my life changing overnight.

Zoey's and my first attempt to start a new life is short-lived. For the first time, I experience Sean's persistence and determination, as well as his willingness to give me everything I once thought I wanted. He quits drinking immediately and even has a thought-out plan to guarantee results. He promises to take a serious step toward his recovery by applying for an inpatient rehab program and finally turning a page on his addiction. He'll leave almost immediately, leaving Zoey, me, and the house to ourselves for the next couple of weeks. Then we can put the house on the market and move closer to the mountains to adopt a lifestyle more in line with that we've both always wanted.

This is a tempting proposition when I don't know where Zoey and I will sleep the next night. After much negotiating with myself, I agree to give this a chance.

The following Wednesday, I find myself once again on the meditation floor, sobbing. I really don't want to be in this marriage. I no longer want to walk this path with Sean. Every inch of my body, every part of my mind, and every beat of my heart know this. Yet, I don't know how to reconcile that knowing with how the situation around me is shifting.

Am I supposed to stand in my new truth and walk away, or should I seize this opportunity to rebuild our relationship and take a new chance on us? Am I giving up too quickly, or have I had enough?

Lucia's wise words after meditation put my mind at ease.

"You don't need to know. You can keep doing what you're doing until the answer is so clear that you can't help but take action in that direction."

It doesn't take long for the truth to stare at me in the face. Sean and I haven't said a nice thing to each other in years. I can't remember the last time we were intimate. We have abused our marriage to the point of no return—recovering from addiction won't bridge this gap we've built between us. The years of rejection, neglect, and pushing each other away have worn out our hearts. We've had years of dysfunction and grown further and further apart. Changing one factor is not going to fix the whole thing. And to be honest, I don't have the energy to try to fix anything anymore.

Chapter Three

*I*WAIT FOR SEAN to get back from rehab, a ticket to New York in hand. Conveniently, I have to travel for business for a few days. I honestly don't remember how well I masked my relief to get away. I haven't really had any alone time since coming back from Stella's. I've ridden a rollercoaster of emotions trying to manage a new situation that I still don't want. The internal back and forth as to how to move forward is exhausting.

On my eastbound flight, I fantasize about walking the streets of NYC aimlessly, getting lost among the skyscrapers, with no one to carry along. I love many things about the Big Apple, but one of its most appealing is the anonymity of being in a city with over eight million people. Every New York minute, the busyness of the city masks any one individual action. As a visitor, you can arrive and leave without anyone noticing you were ever there. As soon as you cross the first street, you get swallowed up into a sea of people.

In NYC, I don't have to be anyone. I don't have to give

anything. No one there expects anything from me, other than a straightforward answer. I've tried to go the extra mile and smile at people walking by me on the street, only to find it completely unnecessary. Most people don't seem to know what to do with it. Besides, after being stuck in an internal whirlwind for weeks, I don't want to smile unless it's real. I don't want to pretend I am doing okay. I just want everything to wash off me—the last few years of my marriage, the past, the new layer of pain I have found. Maybe I can even muster the courage to face my fear of the change I need to make.

I walk (almost skip) to my work meeting the first day in the city, feeling the rush of winter on my face. I just need to feel myself, to be myself. I feel more alive than I have in a very long time. I enjoy a great solo dinner and even make it to a musical on Broadway. I feel free and relieved.

Back in my hotel room, I call home. Sean answers after a few rings, and I can immediately tell he's too inebriated to even keep a conversation straight.

Zoey is crying in the background, and I can't find out why. I feel so guilty to have spent a day taking care of myself when my three-year-old daughter has no one to take care of her. Was I crazy to leave them alone and trust that he could stay sober for three days? We had just invested in his recovery, and here he was relapsing—again.

But it isn't really his relapse that upsets me. What *really* gets me is the fact that I'm still kidding myself. I still think things are magically going to work out. Worse than the years of trying to force things forward, I've spent the last month being paralyzed and just standing by. I keep denying myself of what I really want, which is to get myself and Zoey the hell out of this situation. I don't want this to be my life anymore. I want to create something new that's true to what I want for Zoey and me. But this is not the time to have this tantrum or to figure all of that out.

I know Sean can't take care of Zoey tonight. It's only 6:00 p.m., and I fear things will get worse before her bedtime. Containing my rage so I can make a sound decision, I call Lucia. She drops what she's doing to help us.

"Lucia, I need you to go get Zoey. Sean is drunk and can't take care of her. I'm in New York and will get on the next flight."

"Leaving my house now. I'll let you know when I have her."

"Thank you. Please take her to Stella's. She can stay there for the night, and I'll be back in the morning."

Lucia tells me later that Sean just stood there and watched her pack Zoey's things and drive away. I'm grateful there seems to be an implicit agreement among all of us that Zoey's safety comes first.

I cancel the rest of my meetings, change my flight, and— once I know Zoey is safe for the night—let myself rest for a couple of hours before heading to the airport to catch a red-eye home.

With all my travel for work, I've gotten used to meditating on planes. I believe it's the most productive way to spend otherwise idle time. Sometimes, I simply listen to some Gregorian chants and sink within. Other times, I listen to talks by my Spiritual Master to find guidance in an area of my life where I'm facing some challenge or darkness. Many times, I pray. Whichever practice or technique I choose, meditating helps me stay grounded and centered as I fly off to my next destination or let the stress of the trip wash off me on the way home.

On this particular flight home, I need to pray. My prayer is of gratitude. Things seem to be falling apart on the outside. Within, however, everything is starting to fall into place. I don't have to worry about Zoey's safety. I don't have to negotiate with myself any longer. I know what needs to be done.

⚘

I arrive at Stella's house and Zoey welcomes me with what I eventually learn is her signature, everything-is-fine smile. I wrap my arms around her and give her a big squeeze. I don't know how much she understands of what's happened or how her life will completely change next.

Almost like déjà vu, we are back where we were a few short weeks ago: at Stella's house and without a plan. Something is different, however. This time, it's clear we are not going back home. There's no time for grieving, only action.

By mid-morning, I see that Sean has called me dozens of times, presumably to beg me to come back, based on the hundreds of text messages sent in between attempts. I don't want to have that conversation. There is nothing I need to say. Whatever might come out of my mouth would likely be painful for both of us.

By evening, I am calm and finally answer one of his calls, worried that he will send the police otherwise. Instead, I am the one who has to send them. Let me explain.

"It's over," he says.

Part of me is relieved that perhaps, finally, he has realized and accepted that I'm serious this time. He keeps talking, not making much sense. But then he makes it easy to catch up.

"I don't want to live if I can't have a life with you and Zoey."

Now, I'm in full-on reaction mode. I hang up on him and immediately call the police.

"My husband just called me and it sounds like he's thinking about committing suicide. Please stop him!" I say and give them our home address.

Without thinking twice, I grab my jacket and get ready to jump in the car. Before I hop in, Stella stops me in my tracks and asks me to walk with her first. I find this odd, but I also know I need to calm down if I want to make it there safely.

"Why do you want to drive over there?" she asks.

"I don't know," I say. "I just think I need to be there. I need to stop him."

"I've never heard of anyone who said they were going to commit suicide who actually did it. I can almost guarantee he's just trying to get a reaction out of you. You're forty-five minutes away. If he's really going to do it, it will be done by the time you get there. What's the point?" she says as her contagious calmness gives me permission to take a deep breath.

What would I do if I got there and found he had done it anyway?

That deep breath is what I needed for common sense to kick into gear. Then, the internal battle restarts.

What needs to happen for him in this moment is really just part of his path. I don't have to fix things for him anymore. I need to finally move on, and he needs to make his own decisions.

Although I know this is the truth, these are hard thoughts for me to reconcile.

How can I not show up for the man I've spent the last

seven years with?

I have been his safety net for long enough. Every time he was about to do something stupid, I found a way to stop him.

This back-and-forth drones on as I wrestle with making my decision. Later in my journey I'll learn that this is a conversation between my mind and my awareness. My mind follows known patterns, guided by conditioning and trauma—what I've been told is the right thing to do according to social norms and unfortunate interactions I've had along the way. But Truth, I've learned, doesn't come from my mind. There's a deeper place inside where the guidance isn't corrupted and God can show me a new path that isn't born of pressure and struggle. I just have to be willing to listen.

Taking a walk with Stella helps me see that this kind of mental ping-ponging is exactly the reason I'm constantly exhausted and depleted. I sit down and wait for news, as I comfort Zoey. This is where I need to be.

Within fifteen minutes, I don't just hear from the police—I also hear from our real estate agent. A family that was looking to buy our house had stopped by for an inspection. But that deal is dead now. They were, understandably, freaked out and turned off. As the police barged into our home, Sean was at the bar around the corner, having a drink. And this is our marriage in a nutshell. He would talk about doing something, then never see it all the way through. When that happened—whether it was about his addiction, like this time, or something else—he always hoped to get a reaction out of me. And that's exactly what he would get. I would stress out as I worked diligently to solve the problem, then wind up exhausted and resentful. But now, I'm through with this.

❦

The next morning, I open a new bank account, reroute my paycheck, contact a divorce lawyer, enroll Zoey into a new daycare close to Stella's house, and start looking for a new home—all within a matter of hours.

The next time I see Sean is at our divorce mediation. He looks like he hasn't been getting a lot of sleep. I am focused on the end goal, and it's likely the coldest he's ever seen me. Like a soldier ready to go to battle, I have a clear plan to execute to protect Zoey and myself. I care less about who gets which piece of furniture.

Sean will have to prove that he won't drink while Zoey is under his supervision for three whole months before she can stay with him overnight. He can spend time with her during the day but has to return her to me before his "weak hour," when drinking becomes the only possible relief for his pain. With every relapse, the clock would reset, and he would have to prove himself for another three months. It's a testament of how much he loves Zoey—or perhaps how defeated he feels— that he accepts every term I put forward.

In the next few months, some things stay the same, like Zoey's and my evening walks to the park. Some things are new, such as friends stopping by unannounced to bring us delicious dinners. In theory, I have more work to do because everything now falls on my shoulders. In reality, the load feels lighter, as I no longer have to drag anyone along.

The sale of our home is the only thing about our divorce that moves quickly, but only because that process had already begun, and stopping it would have required some serious effort on Sean's end. The rest takes nearly a year. Sean's new in-patient rehabilitation program becomes the perfect excuse, as it is hard to reach him, especially in his delicate emotional state. When he finally returns home, he is sure to remind me that getting divorced was never a mutual decision and that he refuses to participate. It's become clear that I am solely responsible for keeping track of everything divorce related.

As our path forward becomes clearer and clearer for me, Sean seems more confused. What were sharp, painful memories to me seem to have become increasingly blurred incidents to him. He expresses how he is absolutely clueless about why exactly I left. He says he thinks I've changed. I know I have.

As I look back now, I recognize that we were both trying to find closure and heal in that tugging and pulling. We were both trying to make sense of our new reality. I don't think either of us wished to magically find happiness, but we didn't want to feel like we had failed.

I'm not sure many people understand what it means to have a broken family. We get caught up in our individual trauma and pettiness, and when we finally realize the whole thing has burst at the seams, all that's left is lots of cleaning up and picking up the pieces. It's painful, and no one wins.

I wasn't all of a sudden feeling amazing and free. Just like Sean, I had lost the marriage and family I had been trying to build for the last seven years. He would have it a lot worse, losing it all many more times into the future. And Zoey, in many ways, was along for the ride. Neither Sean nor I could ever repair the past, but we could prevent further damage in the future. That was at least my commitment.

Chapter Four

Every week, for months after Zoey and I permanently moved out, I show up at the meditation center on Wednesday nights, sit on the meditation floor and collapse into tears. Without fail, I have something new to cry about every week. If it isn't Sean calling and texting incessantly with messages about how I am the worst person in the world or how he can't live without me, it is my exhaustion from full-time parenting, or Zoey's latest heartbreaking therapy session.

Then, there was that day I got a different call. This time it wasn't from the police or the rehab center. It was instead from the hospital. Sean had had a seizure and hit his head on a desk on his way to the ground. Although I had been consistently meditating and emptying out my mind and heart, I felt ready to explode at the news. I was immediately overwhelmed by thoughts about whether he'd be okay or whether he might have a similar incident while driving Zoey in the car. Also, why in the world was I still his emergency contact? I couldn't take it.

That night, I walked into the meditation room, curled up into a little ball on the floor, and lost it. There was no room to be grateful for having that space at the time but looking back I now see how this community and practice have been a godsend.

As I sobbed, I prayed and begged.

"Who the hell will hold me?"

I didn't have a partner. My family lived in a different hemisphere. My friends had their own lives. Besides, who wants to hang out with someone immersed in this kind of never-ending drama?

I wasn't expecting a miracle where the church ceiling opened for God's mighty hand to descend in a healing beam of light. But if I'm being honest, perhaps I was delirious enough to hope that I would feel His love wrap around me somehow. His actual response was much more subtle.

I felt our meditation teacher walk over. She kneeled down on the floor and held me. I don't know whether she knew I needed to be held or whether God asked her to do it. All I know is that I got the hug I longed for. In that moment, it didn't matter where it came from. What was important was that it came as warm, tight, and loving as I needed it to be.

That night, her (or His?) embrace taught me it's not that no one is listening, but that I need to be prepared for what I'm asking for to come in a form I may not have expected. In fact, I might get just what I need in a much better way if I'm open-minded and just surrender.

This awareness filled me with new joy. I started seeing how many of the things I had prayed for were in my life already, perhaps not how I thought, but the outcome was the same. I wanted to raise Zoey in a loving environment, and we were now surrounded by great love from our friends. I had begged for help reconnecting with my passion, and I now had the freedom to go dancing if I just booked a babysitter. I had prayed for a new lifestyle, and my divorce resulted in me moving closer to my friends and living a peaceful life in the mountains, close to rivers and beautiful trails.

It's a few weeks after that day when I was divinely held on the meditation floor, and I'm having dinner at a restaurant with a friend. Then, that peaceful life, born of open-mindedness as to how God would hold us next, gets tested in a significant way.

I was hesitant to let Zoey stay with Sean overnight, but I had already stretched my rights as a co-parent to keep my daughter safe. He had also been flexible and understanding enough to play along with each one of my rules and requests about how to care for her. I still dreaded she might experience abuse or neglect as I dropped her off and walked away each time. That afternoon, I said goodbye and left with a prayer in my heart that she would be protected.

As I await my entrée, I'm surprised to see a call from Sean past Zoey's bedtime. I answer the call skeptically, hoping this isn't one of those times when he wants to express just how much he loves or hates me. Instead, I hear Zoey's tiny, cracking voice.

"Mommy, no one's taking care of me. Daddy is asleep on the couch, and I can't wake him up," she tells me as she sniffs in her tears.

I stand up and leave the table and my friend, spouting half a story about why I'm bolting. I stay on the phone with my four-year-old daughter for the next twenty minutes as I run to my car and drive to her dad's house. I want to keep her entertained and reassure her that she isn't alone, so we sing songs together and plan what we'll have for dinner. I also can't help but tell her repeatedly how much I love her and am so incredibly sorry this is happening.

As I pull up to Sean's house, I see the front door wide open. Zoey is standing in the doorway, waiting for me. I take a deep breath, put on a smile, get out of the car, and walk up the steps to meet her tiny arms. Sean is, in fact, asleep on the couch, with more cans of beer on the coffee table than I care to count. I try to wake him up. Unsuccessful, I gather Zoey's things, strap her into her car seat, and drive home.

As I'm still processing how I feel about the situation the next morning, Zoey surprises me with a very mature reflection.

"Mom, it's not okay for daddy to not take care of me. I was scared. Just like that time he went to get more beer and left me alone."

For a while now, I've been encouraging her to put words to her feelings as a way to process them. I've encouraged her to speak up when something doesn't feel right. While there's trauma I can't control, I can at least help her respond healthily. Now that guidance is paying off. Next she tells me she's hesitant to go back to her dad's house because she doesn't want this to happen again.

"You're right, Zoey. It's not okay that you were left alone, with no one there to feed you dinner or make sure you were safe. You're a child, and our job as parents is to take care of you. Would you like to tell your dad how you feel?" I say, hoping to empower her to set boundaries and learn to use her voice.

She takes me up on the offer, and my heart jumps with

joy. No, this isn't a happy moment by most standards, but something more important is happening. I know what it's like to undo years of being silenced and having boundaries not being respected. I'm learning to use my voice myself, and it's never too early to start. I didn't need to shine a light on how her dad was irresponsible or a bad parent. She came to her own conclusions about the situation. All I need to do is facilitate the outlet for her to find some closure.

Before I can contact her dad to set up some time to talk, my phone rings. He's confused and terrified.

"Did you take Zoey? I can't remember what happened," he cries.

I explain what happened, providing every detail as if he hadn't been there.

"I can't trust you anymore, Sean. But more importantly, Zoey needs to talk to you. In person."

And so she did.

Before Sean went into an inpatient addiction recovery program in a desperate attempt to save our marriage, I supported him through an in-home rehab plan while I was pregnant. As a co-dependent, I was assigned a movie to watch, which explained how addiction works. In the movie, there's a scene in which a cowboy walks into a bar and asks the bartender for a shot of whiskey. The moment the man on the other side of the counter hands it to him, another cowboy walks into the bar and tells Cowboy Number One he will shoot him if he picks up the glass. The camera zooms into Cowboy Number One's mind and guides the viewer through his thought process. In that moment, the part of his brain that is responsible for survival and instinct kicks into gear. Every thought afterward aims at figuring out whether he can get the shot of whiskey down his throat before the bullet hits his brain and kills him.

I never understood the grip addiction could have on even the most intelligent and caring people until I saw that movie. I spent hours explaining to Sean why he needed to make changes and why this drinking habit wasn't good for him or his family. It didn't matter. At the end of the day, his addiction would take over and drive him to single-mindedly focus on acquiring the substance that would provide release from his particular chemical imbalance. No logic or act of love could change that.

This understanding has helped me never again question Sean's adoration for his daughter. When he's sober, he's a loving and caring father. He plans fun activities and looks forward to seeing her. But when he's under the influence, the demons of his disease are stronger than love and good intentions.

A year after I had taken a red-eye back from New York, things look different on the surface. We have separate houses and barely talk to each other. If you look deeper, however, you'll see we are still legally married, he is still drinking, and I am still in a constant state of panic, waiting for the next wave of bad news or the next traumatic situation to unfold. And now I'm due to return to New York.

Something else is different this time, though. I've left Zoey with her very trustworthy babysitter, knowing she will be safe with her. Now I walk the streets of NYC, hoping for the same sense of freedom I had felt when I first visited the city ten years ago. But my relationship with NYC has been tainted by the phone call that sent me rushing home last time, and I can't shake the feeling that some new problem might come out of nowhere.

I do my best to dismiss those thoughts, telling myself there's no need to be paranoid. But just after getting comfortable enough to venture out for some good coffee, I get an unexpected call from Zoey's therapist, kindly calling to inform me that she had just reported us to Child Protective Services. What is it with me and New York?

My beaten-down heart takes the punch one more time as my mind searches for answers to all my confused, panicky questions. Nothing. I have no idea what this means. Crying, I ask what I should expect. Would the police show up to her school or my home and take her while I was away, no questions asked?

The therapist told me that Zoey had discussed the incident about her dad falling asleep on the couch. Understandably, she had to report it. I ask follow-up questions about how to best handle the situation moving forward and how to empower Zoey to process the trauma, but I still feel helpless.

"I'm not coming home for another day," I tell her. "I don't know how these things work. Will she be taken away from me?"

"I don't know what will happen. You will likely be contacted." That is not the response I expected from a professional.

"I'm not the one who neglected her. I was only letting him exercise his parental rights. Why would they take her away from me?"

No answers.

I immediately contact Stella and Lucia, asking them to once again hold Zoey. I didn't know if it was okay for Zoey to be with a babysitter. Would Child Services consider that neglect as well? Or would they understand that I had to travel for my job so I could provide for her? I am so clueless. The suspense tortures me for the next twelve hours as I await my flight home. In the meantime, I ask her dad to stay away. We can't risk both of us losing her.

My fast-tracked return proves unnecessary, but I do get a call from Child Services a week later. They want to see my home, especially Zoey's bedroom, and to interview me and her separately so they can evaluate whether I am a safe parent. Luckily, I pass the test.

I'll never know whether fear or a true altruistic desire drove Sean to attempt to turn the ship once and for all, but this series of events has reignited Sean's interest in pursuing recovery. As my home and parenting style were being investigated, he conveniently left for yet another in-patient program before the social worker's visit was even over.

Sean apparently got the call from Child Services weeks later when he was already in the rehab center and somewhat sheltered from any potential consequences. Child Services deemed this proof enough that he was working on his recovery and closed the case. Just like that. The social worker assigned to our case later explained, "She's staying with you now, and her dad is in rehab, so there's not much we can do."

I feel absolutely failed by the system, and the lack of true care for my daughter. Am I supposed to continue to put Zoey into potentially dangerous situations until something bad enough happens for the law to intervene? It feels like I'm playing Russian roulette with my daughter's life, but do I have a choice?

Chapter Five

SOON ENOUGH, ZOEY AND I are back into our routine. No matter how exhausting single parenting can be, it somehow feels easier than co-parenting. With Sean in rehab, I have control over my daughter's safety (when she's with me), my time off, and our schedule. I continue to gain strength with every meditation and retreat. I have adopted a new morning routine that includes letting go of worries and negative thoughts—I listen to music and dance like no one is watching. This helps me start the day with a positive attitude and feel ready to continue building a good life for us.

But the thought of Sean coming out of rehab (once again) concerns me. I'm tired of the back-and-forth. I don't want to find out how the next chapter of his life impacts ours. I want Zoey and I to have a choice about his involvement in our lives. But, like a boomerang, he returns wanting to engage more than ever before.

Although I appreciate the effort and really want to have compassion for his situation, the truth is I'm resentful. Yes, he offers to share the load of parenting by having Zoey over, which would mean more free time and less to pay for. But I think I'd rather pay my way to freedom by hiring a babysitter so I can stay in control. I'm not proud of how my controlling nature has been laid bare, but I have made more emergency runs home from work trips and dinners than I would like.

In an effort to loosen up and let go of some control, I tell Sean he's welcome to pick Zoey up from school and have her overnight. I have a work dinner, and he's been begging to spend time with her. He just needs to give her dinner, put her to bed, and get her to school safely the next morning. Straightforward enough. So, once again, I trust—but not without saying that prayer again, "Please, God, keep her safe." Once again, God listens and intervenes, albeit not in the way I would have expected.

As I walk into the restaurant with my co-workers, I get one of those "Unknown" calls I've come to dread. It's the police. On the way to pick up Zoey from school, Sean gets into an accident on the highway. When the police show up, he receives a DUI, and another charge for gun possession under the influence.

There is, once again, no time to think and only one thing to do—rush to my daughter. Perhaps the title of this story should have been *Life Interrupted*, because that's what my life has looked like for the past couple of years.

This time, Sean ends up in jail. On top of taking care of Zoey by myself, I now have something new to worry about: how will being incarcerated impact Sean emotionally and psychologically? But I don't have to wonder for long, because he shares his experiences on the inside in his letters to Zoey.

I'll spare the details to respect my ex-husband's privacy,

but it suffices to say that the content of the letters is at times beyond my daughter's maturity level. While I appreciate how this experience has allowed him to reflect on his previous actions, I don't believe my five-year-old daughter needs to hear about every one of her father's epiphanies.

Now, I don't believe in lying to my daughter or even sugarcoating things, no matter her age. I believe trust is built when we witness honesty. So, I do my best to speak the truth and help her understand what her father is saying to her, even when I absolutely dread saying it out loud. I can't risk losing Zoey's trust when so much of her world is falling apart. I'm not going to perpetuate my daughter's suffering by dressing up what is happening now. Offering age-appropriate, bite-sized information seems one way I can help, but it seems just as important to filter out Sean's depressing thoughts and feelings about the type of father he wished he had been. One day, she'll have a chance to read every word and come to her own conclusions. At that point, I may need to explain myself and my rationale for handling things this way.

My Spiritual Master says everyone wants to know the truth. Yet, I can see the wheels turning in the head of every person who learns Sean is in jail. Without fail, they ask, "What have you told Zoey?"

"The truth," I reply each time.

Here's the thing. Society has expectations of every one of its members, but mothers' decisions and actions are particularly scrutinized. I sort of get it. After all, we *are* raising the next generation of human beings. It's sort of a big deal. As a species, our love and support of others is completely conditional and dictated by our own concepts, perceptions, and beliefs about how things should be. Everyone feels entitled to opinions and even judgements, and we tend to affiliate with those who think or live the same way as us.

As these events have unfolded in my life, I've started to challenge myself to go beyond this instinct and test my initial gut reaction against the more sound compass I have recently found within. This has helped me get a better sense of what's true for me, especially related to being a mother.

One of the greatest benefits of meditation is that it provides distance between the self and our thoughts and emotions. It allows us to take a step back as we let our thoughts float away and our feelings burn off, so all that's left is what is. It doesn't always mean that I like what I find on the other side of the whirlwind, but, in my experience, it is a much more objective perspective.

Here's an example of one of those times when I really didn't like what was on the other side.

My friend Stella had been a rock in my life, always welcoming Zoey and I into her home and having my back whenever the next crisis hit. She was like a sister to me. When she asked why I was still choosing a job that took me away from my daughter a couple of days every other week and expressed reservations about me spending so much time meditating, I listened. Or, more accurately, I judged and doubted myself. I didn't know if I was making the right decisions.

Was it okay for me to continue pursuing my career? Was I investing too much time and money into my spiritual growth? Did this new lifestyle make me a bad mom? There's no manual for this.

As I had done for the past few years, I took this to the meditation floor to find some answers. Underneath the judgement was anger and resentment. I let myself feel it all. I cried. I screamed. I shook my head until all the negative thoughts left me. When I felt that it was time to calm down, I sat down and took some deep breaths, telling my heart it was time to slow down. My mind was still, and I could ask some old and new questions to find clarity.

Was I handling things the right way? Was I making a mistake by spending time meditating for my mental health? Was this the wrong job for me to have while all this was going on? Should I give up on what I want for myself? Would that be a worthwhile sacrifice for Zoey's benefit, or would I be trying to check all the boxes of what someone else thought a mother should do? Was I not simply putting the oxygen mask on first, just as the flight attendants always say to do? Was I being selfish? Should I have given up on the idea of having a career as a single mother? Was I neglecting Zoey in any way? How else would I provide for her? Should I have focused on my happiness, Zoey's happiness, or making everyone else happy?

Without doubt, judgment, resentment, and anger coloring my view, I could feel my body responding to each of these questions and more. Answers didn't come in the form of words. Instead, I felt the truth about the situation become clear in my body and heart.

This spiritual work and my hours of meditation were the biggest gifts I'd ever given to myself—and Zoey. I needed them to keep sane in the midst of the chaos we'd endured. I also needed the financial stability my current job provided to be able to support my daughter. I needed money to not be an issue, because there were too many other things for me to solve and worry about. I knew that if I didn't keep going deeper into myself and really let go of every insecurity and negative belief that had gotten me entangled in my current suffering and struggle, I wouldn't be able to move forward. Worse, I wouldn't be able to support Zoey on her own already convoluted journey.

From that point on, I started taking everyone's opinion with a grain of salt. I listened to feedback and was open-minded enough to ask myself the questions people asked of me. I never based my life solely on what someone else thought I should be doing. As much as I loved Stella, her perspective was coming from a set of completely different circumstances. She hadn't worked since becoming pregnant with her then seven-year-old daughter. She had a loving husband who took care of her in every possible way. She didn't have the same worries I did. I was happy for her, but I needed to stay true to my path, my needs, and my daughter's needs in our particular situation.

This realization didn't create distance within us initially, although I did feel more grounded in my decisions. We continued to be friends, and I supported her as she went through health issues, just like she had supported me when my marriage fell apart. Then, there was a defining moment in our relationship.

One afternoon, as I packed my suitcase to leave on a trip the next day, I got a call from Sean. He had been released from jail a couple of months before and was now on probation, which allowed him to spend more time with Zoey and keep her overnight. However, he had just been given a new sentence and had to go back.

I should have known better than to think I could rely on Sean. Instead, I had planned a business trip, counting on him taking care of Zoey while I was away. I had to leave the next morning, and now my plans had changed. As I booked the babysitter and got everything ready for Zoey to be home with her for a couple of nights, Stella messaged me, asking for a favor she needed that very afternoon. I sincerely felt I couldn't add one more thing to my schedule. I had to choose Zoey and my sanity.

I asked if I could do it later in the week. And, before I could explain why, she never spoke to me again. After all she had done for us, I can see how not dropping everything to help her in that moment may have seemed selfish or that we were ungrateful. I still wish I could have shown up for her that day, but I've had to let go of that guilt.

Since then, I've had to walk away from other situations without feeling the need to explain and justify myself, accepting that certain doors will close and that all I can do is stay true to myself, knowing I'm doing the best I can. This has forced me to be uncomfortably honest about whether I am acting from a place of love and what I know to be true at that point. That's the only way I can find some peace.

I had to let go of our friendship, and in the process, I got to reflect on what being a good friend really means. I now understand that true friendship is not about making my friend happy or doing only what they approve of. A friendship is a choice for two people to walk individual paths by each other's side. It means being supportive even when we don't understand or would do it so differently. A friendship is a commitment to serve as a sounding board when we're needed, as well as letting the other make the mistakes they need to make.

Stella probably thought my not helping her in that moment was a mistake. But this experience has taught me that a friendship is not measured by how often we're able to help with what our friend needs, exactly when they need it. We're allowed to set boundaries in friendships, just as we can do in other relationships. Sometimes, we're the only ones who understand our reasoning, and that's okay. The only true test is whether the reason is born of love and care.

I won't always make the best decisions and may one day look back on this to find I made a mistake. But if I've been diligent enough to go within and question my intention in every decision—not with judgement but with curiosity—then I can trust that I am acting the best way I can in my current awareness and with the deepest love I'm capable of giving to myself and others in that moment.

I love going on walks, especially when I get to follow the river down the mountain and through my small town. There are big boulders all along the path, each one the perfect spot to sit down, hear the water run, feel the breeze tickle the leaves behind me, and read a book or just leave it all behind for a moment. Stella and I used to go there together. I miss her.

Being at peace with the choices I've made helps calm my mind. But my heart aches. A part of me still wishes I could have given Stella exactly what she wanted. I wish I could do that for every person in my life. We all deserve love. I walk the trail alone this time, and I can't help but let tears roll down my cheeks.

Is it possible to try to make everyone happy? What do I have to give? When do I give too much? When do I not give enough?

I choose a rock by the water and sit down. I close my eyes, and as I feel my unworthiness and self-judgment creeping in, something more powerful whispers in my ear.

All this time, I've believed fixing things for others is what I have to give. I'm the first one to raise my hand to volunteer for an extra project at work. If a friend asks for something, I cancel my plans to make it happen. I will overbook myself and not leave time for me, even to simply rest.

And this, ladies and gentlemen, is how I assign worth and value to myself. I do this because I care and have a good heart, yes. But also, I do this because I feel helpful and proactive, and my ego gets a kick out of "doing the right thing for others." I have a belief that my worth is directly proportionate to how much I feel I've sacrificed or given.

One of my Spiritual Master's most powerful teachings is that we are all beautiful gems. She speaks about why none of us are worthy and valuable because of our actions. Making mistakes doesn't make us less worthy either. We are born and will die worthy of love. The rest is icing on the cake.

With this in mind, I imagine a world where I start saying no—not because I'm planning to become selfish and stop giving all of a sudden, but because I only have so many resources. Every single resource on this material plane is limited. That's the nature of how things are.

From this new awareness, I start keeping track of how I use my resources. I start by considering the basics required to provide for Zoey. There's time for work, then time for chores to keep the house and our life in order. Then, there's quality time with my daughter. I also need time to nurture myself for my own sanity, whether that's through meditating, hanging out with friends, or going for a walk. After adding all that time up, what is left is what I have to give.

But this isn't a zero-sum game and I can't always give the same things to people. Fulfilling the needs of Zoey, myself, and my co-workers also involves giving, so it's not like I would ever break even anyway. Some days, taking care of my main obligations takes up all my resources. Other days, once I've found time to meditate and am filled with joy, I get a second wind and have the capacity to pay it forward in some unexpected way.

Before I tried to get my life into balance, there was a part of me that just wanted to be isolated, to check out. I wanted to watch TV and not really worry about things. I didn't want to clean my house. I didn't want to do the dishes.

If I'm being honest, I was resentful that I had to take care of everything in my daughter's and my lives. I was exhausted probably because I was working like a maniac. I would come home and just be absolutely stressed out and maxed out. I didn't have the capacity to take care of everything that needed to be done.

I couldn't name the underlying feeling driving my attitude at the time. All I knew was that I was pissed off. I started blaming my ex-husband. How dare he leave me alone with our daughter! He just expected me to deal with the consequences of his actions, pick up the pieces, and fully take over the care of our daughter.

With his DUI and my losing contact with Stella, I didn't know when or how I would find some relief. What I did know is that I was absolutely done riding everyone else's rollercoaster. To avoid that, I trained myself to become the biggest doer, always ready to tackle the next project and get it all the way to the finish line. Every. Time. I didn't let myself rest or rely on others. I couldn't trust others to create the right circumstances to ensure my success. I had bought into the belief that lack of control was dangerous, so I did all I could to ensure every outcome, which burned me out in the end.

At this time in my life, there were too many factors I couldn't control. I didn't know what the answer was. I did know there was a part of me that was exhausting me, trying to somehow hold it all together. One of the first things I lost control of was my pain. I was constantly feeling all kinds of emotions, and I was sick of meditating just so I could release the last twenty-four hours of chaos—and then start all over again the next day.

Since finding more balance and accepting how my relationship with Stella changed, I've learned that the path of self-discovery is one of letting go and finding freedom. As my Spiritual Master teaches us, every realization and every new layer of awareness provides light. This light, in turn, illuminates a new area of darkness. Darkness was what I was facing as she encouraged me to be grateful. Now, with my light, I see a new path to follow.

Chapter Six

ERE I AM AGAIN at the meditation center for yet another retreat. Five days with nothing else to do besides going within and facing what's inside and ahead of me. My resistance is tangible. My exhaustion has convinced me that I'm a victim of my own life. I have so many circumstances and people around me to blame for how my life has turned out.

First chance I get, I complain and sob about how I've ruined everything for my daughter and myself. I feel lost and don't know where to go next. I don't know how to make the avalanche stop or how to get off the roller coaster. I divorced Sean so I wouldn't have to carry the weight of him and his addiction. And here I am, still entangled in his drama, letting it impact Zoey's and my life. He's not doing anything *to* me, but that's how it feels.

As I sit there on the meditation floor, feeling sorry for myself and whining endlessly about how crappy my life is, I get guidance from one of my spiritual teachers:

"Even if you are successful at removing every single situation that causes you and your daughter's pain from your life, you and she will still experience pain. We live in a world of duality—there's darkness and light. And the reality is, the darkness will never go away. Assume that the darkness will always be there, and still find the light. More importantly, hold the light and let it illuminate your response to what is. That's all you can control."

First, I feel challenged and want to argue with him. Then, even though I don't fully know what that means, I recognize it as truth. In that moment, I see clearly that I've been trying to control how much darkness surrounds Zoey and me. It's sort of ridiculous and, frankly, arrogant.

My spiritual teacher asks me why I can't just let go.

"Just put it into God's hands and ask for the suffering to be taken away from you."

This is terrifying territory for me. Can I trust it? Can I trust Him?

I go into a deep meditation. As I feel little bubbles of feelings popping up inside, I explore them, curiously. As I place my attention on them, they burst, and I'm fully in that feeling. I go into the rage and punch a pillow. I go into the sadness and scream as I sob. I go into my deep longing for all the suffering to just go away. I can't get myself to hand it over, though. I'm still stuck feeling that I can do it all on my own, if I just try hard enough. Then there's that exhaustion again. I surrender and beg deeply. "Please take this pain away. I no longer want this. This is too hard." I think I'm talking to God, but my words are there for anyone who'll listen.

In my exhaustion, I'm shown the strength that lives inside me. I can feel it in my heart and my vigilance, in my commitment to get out of the shadows as many times as it takes. I have been holding more than I ever knew I could. I just hadn't had a moment to take a deep breath and be compassionate to myself. I always keep pushing and never accept or—even more taboo for a strong woman like me—ask for help.

This realization is accompanied by a feeling of gratitude and relief. Yes, things are messed up. No, I don't have control over what my ex-husband does. But I do have my freedom. My freedom isn't dependent on what happens when my ex-husband wakes up every day. It is dependent on how I react to and work with the circumstances.

When am I choosing to engage when I don't have to? What am I trying to control that I can't control? What is up to me? What is my part in all of this? Why am I driving myself absolutely nuts trying to create a parallel reality rather than working with this one?

For the first time, I start grasping the idea of accepting what is. And I find a way to be in that acceptance that doesn't look like being resigned. I understand that acceptance is not just saying, "Well, this is just the way it is, and there's nothing I can do about it." Accepting is finally saying, "I see you, darkness, and I am not going to engage," and having the humility to know that I don't know the bigger picture. In fact, what is currently happening may be exactly what needs to happen right now. Understanding that I actually have that power to choose is incredibly helpful and liberating for me. Those divorce papers did very clearly imply I no longer have to catch Sean every time he falls. Now I see I don't have to do that for anyone else either.

Except my daughter, of course. But that is a choice I've

made. I have committed myself to supporting her, and that means also taking action when that is appropriate. Taking her to therapy so she can process her pain. Making sure she has everything she needs to be successful in her education. I am doing so much already, but all this time I have only focused on what I couldn't do or change.

In some ways, I can only guide and provide her with the right tools. But it's not in my power whether she processes her pain or not. In the end, her soul will need to go through its own journey, and I need to trust that God's got her and that she's getting exactly what she needs to find her own freedom. This realization helps me focus on the things that really matter— keeping her safe, caring for her, and giving her my love.

As I peel back the layers in meditation, I realize I've been trying to do it all. No wonder I am exhausted.

I have been keeping my head above water because I'm not just taking in what is happening. I'm taking in the worry, the sense of responsibility to solve problems, the feeling that I have to hold everyone. Then, I still have to show up to work and make sure I'm doing a good job while also trying to be a good friend, mother, and ex-wife.

I've been trying to become Superwoman by trying to hold it all and make sure everything eventually goes smoothly. I'm constantly hoping things just get back on track at some point, and then we can all live happily ever after.

As soon as I let go of the thought that things will somehow magically change, I finally understand what my friend Lucia means when she tells me, "This may not be the worst thing.

There may be something else that's coming that you don't even know about."

I've always judged her as being negative. Why would she say that? Then, it hits me. I haven't surrendered to my destiny. I haven't surrendered to my path and the fact that all of this is what is needed to happen in my life. Because of this, I can't be open and ready to face the next thing head on, holding the light in hand as my Spiritual Master has guided me. Instead, I set myself up for disappointment and let it weaken me. Defeated before the battle starts, I can't move on.

I finally understand a deeper reason why I married my ex-husband: my soul needed to go through this experience so I could learn and find more freedom in this world of illusion. I now know I can't fight every single thing that happens in my life. I understand that God is always painting my canvas. There's something that my soul needs to go through in this lifetime, and those exact circumstances are perfectly and miraculously presenting themselves. And then it's my job to see, observe, and learn how to act from a truer place of love each time, all while letting go of my controlling, arrogant ways.

With this new perspective, I come out of the retreat wanting to try something new. When things happen, I take a deep breath and ask myself, "What do I need to let go of? What needs to be done now? What is the next most urgent thing? What is my ego wanting to do just so I can feel valued?"

There are, it turns out, a few things I can control from this new place:

How I engage in the chaos of life.

How I take care of my mind.

How I care for my body.

How I take care of my heart.

How I love my daughter.

I don't have to get myself into trying situations. I don't have to try to solve everything. I don't need to take on the next challenge. What I need to face will present itself.

The more I let go, the less crazy life feels. I learn that when I'm not holding on so tight, things can flow more easily. I am able to do what needs to be done without feeling guilty about what else could be done. I feel somewhat vulnerable, as I depend more on praying and trusting than being busy trying to fix everything. I do this for my own sanity, even if I am left more exposed than I would like. In that trust, answers I cannot come up with on my own are revealed.

I understand now that if I never had the pain associated with the journey with my ex-husband, I never would have tried to find a new connection with myself. I would have never embarked on a journey to find something deeper than going through the motions of material life. I've started seeing everything that happened as a blessing. And yes, some of those blessings have come in very messy packages.

Aware that I can't stop things from happening, I ask myself upon every new incident, "What is it that I need to learn now? What do I need to let go of? What action do I need to take?"

Asking these questions is helping me see my contribution to the pain and chaos. I'm often so desperate to have my own time that I've been willing to leave Zoey with her father, even though I worry about her safety. Other times, I've let her sit in front of the TV in the evenings rather than being present with her. The exhaustion and laziness have been winning, and I have been willing to bend my own rules for some peace.

Even with all my progress, I'm disappointed in myself. I know better than to look the other way and neglect what really matters. But the real problem is that I haven't been taking care of myself so I could have the energy to not just survive but thrive—and I don't mean thriving in material terms. I mean thriving as in feeling whole inside.

But I had to start somewhere, and my first dive into self-care was pretty basic and mostly focused on material outcomes. My Spiritual Master teaches us that the way we look has an impact on how we feel. How we feel, in turn, impacts how we show up. It's really not about our body being a certain way, but about honoring ourselves with beauty and care. I've started doing simple things like doing my nails, wearing makeup, and dressing beautifully, even when I really didn't want to, as a reminder to show up versus hide in my misery.

I've also decided to get serious about creating a babysitting budget. What do I need to do to preserve my sanity? What am I willing to give up for that? I look at every expense to see where I've assigned value to things that create more of a burden than freedom.

What does this change look like? Well, going to meditation every week has been paramount, so I now have my babysitter on a schedule to watch my daughter every Wednesday night. I feel most free when I travel and want my daughter to have that experience too, so I've started saving with that goal in mind. For me, going on retreats as often as possible is also a way to get back to sanity and have more to give to Zoey, so I make sure to provide myself the time to attend them.

By default, mothers don't get time to really do much self-care, and it's even harder for single mothers. We have to carve time out but then make it hard for ourselves to enjoy that time by letting the guilt pile on. We neglect ourselves, and when the damage is done, we need to dig ourselves out of a bigger hole. I've learned to start with the small things that I can do consistently and to produce a cumulative effect. Slowly but surely, some of the weight upon me is lifting.

Chapter Seven

UNDOUBTEDLY, I INDULGED IN only perceiving my ex-husband as the bad guy. He had made enough mistakes to justify my position. In fact, I could have written a compelling manifesto about how my daughter and I did not deserve "what he had done to us." I would tell everyone who would be willing to listen and lend their sympathy. Yes, there was some truth to this whole justification, but how was that serving me and my daughter? Did I feel freer every time I complained, or did it make me more upset and make me feel trapped in my situation?

I grew so incredibly bitter that I started resenting anything that had to do with helping him in any way. That included shouldering total responsibility for our daughter as he came in and out of her life. I was exhausted and did not want to take care of the house. I continued to make up excuses about not cooking healthier food or having a crazy mess in every room. I was lazy in the evenings and weekends. I started neglecting my finances and responsibilities. I even lost my driver's license because I forgot to renew my license plate (and then I procrastinated for fear of facing the punishment).

In some ways, this all amounted to the perfect story for me. I was a poor, single mom who had to make sure her daughter could see her father in between rehab and jail, and help her understand what the hell was happening as life's complications piled up. I was the one left to handle questions about what I had "done to her dad" and why I had "decided to destroy our family," as her dad had expressed to her on their rare visits together.

I can still hear myself telling that story over and over again. It turned into my excuse for everything. I didn't realize it at the time, but I could have spent hours talking about him and how terrible he was.

I recently read an article about how dehumanizing a person can prevent us from having compassion for that person. We build the case for how a person who has caused us pain has no right to get any compassion from us. Hitler did that in his campaign. And I did that to my ex-husband. I did it for so long I started believing that he was an evil person and that I was just the victim holding my head above water.

But when you have a serious Spiritual Master's guidance and deep encounters with God, you can't get away with embracing a comforting lie for too long. There was something about my attitude toward Sean that wasn't in line with a spiritual path focused on love. It was time for me to put on my big-girl pants and spend another few days meditating on this until I stopped blaming others.

The focus of our work at the next retreat was our lifestyle. Incredibly triggered about this theme, I felt it was being imposed on me and missed the bigger picture of what I was facing. Going in, I didn't appreciate the teachings and reflection moments geared toward examining how I was living, and completely missed the point. I had something else to work on, or so I thought.

When I was encouraged not to look at what needed to change about my lifestyle in material terms, and rather at where I was creating suffering in my life, the resentment came back strong. This time I even resented feeling that I had to be in that retreat to fix my life.

As we were guided to understand how we each held ourselves back, I got very honest with myself. I didn't like that I had to be fully responsible for my daughter. I didn't like that every aspect of parenting—emotional, financial, physical, and otherwise—fell on my shoulders. For the past few years, Sean only showed up when he could get himself out of his own suffering long enough to take Zoey somewhere fun or have her over for a few nights. Then, he would hit another roadblock, and I was expected to pick up the slack. I was the one washing her clothes, helping with homework, enrolling her in school, and taking her to dance class and therapy.

I had been carrying this responsibility around like a burden and was so incredibly mad at him for "putting me" in that situation. I felt everything that wasn't being taken care of was a direct result of him messing up and me needing to pick up the pieces.

Committed to ending the blame, I took these feelings to the mediation floor. As I felt my deeply rooted rage, I started seeing how this constant feeling was impacting my actions and my attitude about my daughter, and how I didn't truly take care of myself or her. Chores were addressed in a half-hearted way, absent of love. Everything I did was born of resentment.

Everything I did had this underlying feeling that I didn't 'want to' but that I 'had to' do it. Every action perpetuated that energy, so there was always something that I didn't want to do.

Then, it hit me. I adored this little girl, and she was going through so much. Centered in my heart, I could feel how my attitude was impacting Zoey. I could feel what she really wanted from me: to be taken care of and to feel my love. She didn't want to feel like I was just pushing along every day.

I found I was also going through so much. Underneath the anger was a desperate desire to be held and helped. After all, I was still just a girl raising another girl. Somehow this image awakened a sense of compassion for myself. I, too, wanted to be taken care of.

Without knowing where to start, I figured it was best to follow the objectives of the retreat and start modifying our daily routine, even though I still wasn't sure it related to what I was facing. Our Spiritual Master guided us in designing a daily program that aimed for balance and to consciously take care of everything we each needed. While I first wondered who really had time for that, I needed to trust that there was a reason this particular retreat was happening as I dealt with my current block.

The daily program we were presented with involved starting the day in prayer and meditating, then exercising, showering, dressing beautifully, and eating a good breakfast to get ready to honor another day. We were guided to approach work with every action being born of love for ourselves and others. Work, thus, was meant to be an act of giving to ourselves so we didn't have to struggle financially. Every day, it was important to take care of our family and have personal as well as spiritual time. Finding new ways to serve others and planning to get enough hours of rest were as important activities as making time for errands and sharing time with others. The goal was learning to live a God-conscious life—a life where love and care accompanies each action and permeates every free moment, allowing us to be receptive to how our life may need to evolve to attract God's presence to it.

As I built my calendar and weekly schedule to accommodate this comprehensive list, I felt frustrated, especially at the fact that no one seemed to understand me. I am a single mom, in case no one got the memo! How dare my Spiritual Master hand me this list of things to take care of every day! I was resistant and resentful again, which was just perfect.

Here's the thing. I've since learned my Spiritual Master doesn't care whether I like what she has to say, or if I even like her. Her guidance comes from a level of consciousness I have yet to achieve, so no wonder I often don't understand. Not until I do the work, anyway. I certainly didn't understand then.

So, why was I adopting this new lifestyle? Because through this journey, I've learned to not trust my feelings, any sense of discouragement, judgments, and negative thoughts. The truth is only hiding underneath them. I just need to be willing to dig deep enough.

So, for the next thirty days, the internal battle became that between my wanting to let go of unnecessary pain and struggle, and my own ideas about how things should go. The schedule felt hard to follow at times, and I often failed to follow it. But I treated each new day as an opportunity to give myself another chance.

With this mind-set, I wrote this letter to God as a way to

formalize my own internal prayer, hoping He'd show me the way with this:

Dear God,

I want to walk my life every day in sweet and willing surrender to what is, detached from material issues. I need to trust You'll guide me in finding the peace and freedom my soul desires.

Please help me stop crying and whining about my petty, little life. I can't believe how unbelievably attached I am to my suffering.

Take me, use me, break me, change me, until my life is completely infused with Your love.

Sophie

Holding onto this prayer and my new attitude to stop letting chaos run my life and create more suffering, I committed to make changes without excuses. And, change I did.

I made a commitment to adopt one new part of the daily program and take care of one thing in the house every night. I deliberately stopped collapsing into the couch or justifying that it was okay to not take care of things after a long day. I now see how laziness was just an excuse to neglect and sabotage myself. By letting things pile up, I was making things more difficult for myself in the end, leaving no time for the things I love to do.

Now, I'm always trying to identify ways I'm wasting my time and where I can up my game. It isn't just about what I need to start doing, but also about what I need to stop doing. More importantly, none of this is driven by me wanting to be the perfect mom, or someone else watching and judging me. It isn't about bragging with each accomplishment. I do this because I care so deeply about my daughter's and my peace that looking the other way is no longer acceptable.

Every day I try something new thinking about my love for Zoey and myself.

What do we deserve? A clean kitchen ready to make a delicious breakfast in the morning? An afternoon in the park? A game night? Laughter? Connection? A healthy meal? Snuggles?

Every new act of devotion fills my heart with love. I don't even have to try. I just have to have that intention that I'm going to do it for her and for me, because the repercussions of me not being responsible or thoughtful have created more worry and sadness in the end.

At the end of the thirty days, I learned that balance is about focusing the necessary attention on each part of life without neglecting one thing or trying to do it all at once. I learned to make decisions that are balanced and support the bigger picture. This meant letting go of what no longer fit in our lives.

Having learned these lessons, I no longer need to buy into the suffering or the idea that everything is so hard. When I feel burdened, I now feel my feelings about it but then adopt the intention to let go of the heaviness and focus my actions on love, devotion, and care.

My Spiritual Master says that the more we awaken to our desire for truth and love, the more we awaken to consciousness automatically. We become mindful, and we start to pay attention to all the details of our lives. We act in ways that make our lives simple and efficient, so we have more room for love.

I don't want my lifestyle to allow room for chaos, laziness, or lack of care and responsibility. This means that whatever mess shows up, internally or externally, I have to be committed to cleaning it up with care and devotion, knowing this will create more love.

This shift has started manifesting externally in my life. I've decluttered and redecorated both my bedroom and Zoey's bedroom so they can be beautiful spaces for us to rest in. I've gone through my drawers and organized them so I can find matching socks without creating a mess or stressing myself out. Every second I'm not struggling to sort through my messes turns into more time for self-care and to be present with Zoey.

Inevitably, I still get overwhelmed at times, but I now have new tools. I sit down and ask, "What needs my attention first?" instead of walking around aimlessly trying to do it all at once. Taking time to think in an organized and conscious way has made me aware of any decisions I might make out of fear or feeling overstressed.

I've begun asking myself in every situation whether I'm being one hundred percent responsible. Am I truly looking at where I can make an impact rather than trying to fix everything? I've become more committed to finding solutions rather than wasting my time whining about the situation. I see how wallowing in my feelings and blaming others is another sign of laziness. In those moments, I'm really just excusing myself from taking any action.

Being a single mom comes with so many responsibilities. There's a lot to take care of, and it becomes easy to put our fate on external circumstances, not seeing how the familiar track playing in our heads—*I don't have time for this. I don't have time for that. I'm overwhelmed by this. Why does it all fall on me?*—is really a trap that prevents us from moving forward. What if we just take responsibility out of love for ourselves and our children? Perhaps, then, we will have true power. That's what makes us superwomen.

For me, all I had to do was be willing to hold myself accountable to take care of everything physical, emotional, and psychological. I had to be willing to no longer indulge in thinking about how unfair a situation is and instead be ready to take action. Now every moment feels like an opportunity to, instead, be grateful for each moment of joy.

Chapter Eight

M Y TOP PRIORITY HAS always been freedom—to be that cage-free hummingbird. This doesn't mean leaving my daughter behind or not being responsible in my life. To me, it means being free to make choices that support the life I want. I love traveling. I love having time to meditate or lose myself in a good book. I love picnics at the park with my daughter. I love a good concert and dancing in the kitchen with Zoey as I make dinner. But more than anything, I want a life in which I'm not yanked around by my circumstances.

As I've tapped into this energy of freedom, I've found I want to create more of it in my life. This became difficult when Zoey's dad, who had somehow been able to help financially until then, was no longer able to do so. How could I now find the money I needed to not only survive and afford the bare necessities, but do so without struggling? I needed help, so I hired a coach to help me look at my finances in a way that could support all aspects of our lives beyond our material needs and in alignment with my values.

She asked me questions I had never asked myself before, such as "Are there actions you haven't taken because you've been ignoring your money?" and "What is the energetic quality of your financial intention?"

As I started going through my budget and expenses with this new perspective, my laziness and resentment showed up all over my bank statements. In a way, I had been trying to solve everything with money by paying my way out of having to do it all. Not a bad concept in theory, as some things are best outsourced, but my execution was wasteful. I knew that the key wasn't about just throwing money everywhere. It was about really getting organized and spending money on the right things. It was about me figuring out a better way to do it all without draining my resources. I had been ordering takeout way too often and throwing things out when I didn't want to deal with fixing them. This was no way to get my life in order or to support myself. I was just sloppily applying a Band-Aid.

As I reviewed my finances with my coach, I learned how to create a budget that supported the life that I wanted. I realized that I could just focus on the things that really supported me, like getting a babysitter or part-time nanny to take care of my daughter when I had to work. And by identifying all my necessary expenses, I was able to become more mindful about how I spent my disposable income.

I realized that self-care for me was being able to go to retreats and community meditation nights, so I needed to continue making those options possible. I also needed a budget to take care of my body, because it had been seriously neglected. The constant back pain when needing to clean or tidy up the house, I found, had a lot to do with my lack of exercise. But I also realized I absolutely hated cleaning. What's worse, I'm terrible at it, so I hired someone to clean my home a couple times a month, leaving me just to maintain in between visits without becoming drained.

As I took things off my plate, I started looking at areas where I could also add more value. Not only could I take on new, engaging projects at work, I could also attend trainings that set me up for a promotion. With the promotion came the extra money I needed to take care of all of my daughter's needs. This may all sound like it was magically happening, but in every one of these realizations and decisions, I was tangibly making changes, becoming more mindful about how I spent every minute and every dollar. What seemed like small choices and incremental actions toward the goal had a visible, long-term impact.

This new perspective on how to allocate my resources to create the life I wanted for myself and Zoey made me reflect further on my intentions. Was I going overboard with what I would buy? Was I trying to mask my guilt by giving my daughter everything she wanted? These questions uncovered how, to a certain extent, I had fallen into a trap of unconscious consumerism and had been buying things to somehow try to make her happy. None of these material things would fix the void of her dad not being present or me not spending enough quality time with her.

My Spiritual Master says that no soul comes into this world to feel fulfilled through material success and wealth. These forms of satisfaction are superficial ways to cover the much deeper emptiness many of us feel. I've experienced myself how society monetizes our emptiness, and glorifies how our ego attains satisfaction and validation, all by acquiring possessions —even experiences. Like a drug, once we've experienced the high, we want to replicate that over and over again, and we even feel lost without it.

But with every dollar that I spend, I'm placing value on something in my life. Buying material things places value on instant gratification. What has mattered in the end was taming the busyness of my material existence to make space within. Simply sitting in the stillness of that emptiness helps me enter a peace, love and freedom that cannot be found anywhere else.

Sticking with this mind-set still takes conscious practice. Some changes to my budget still allow sneaky guilt to creep in. I catch myself feeling guilty about saying no to my daughter's request for a new toy. But this has allowed me to save money to travel with her, spend quality time together, and create beautiful memories. For a time, I also felt guilty that much of my budget was going to my self-care. But I needed that. I couldn't exhaust every resource with the mind-set that I would only be surviving rather than finding sustainable, long-term support. By caring for myself, I've *created* the support both Zoey and I need.

Still, even as I understand this need to take care of myself, I sometimes feel selfish with each decision tied to this intention. My core false belief that I don't deserve to be loved and cared for has existed in me for longer than I can remember. My lack of self-worth naturally turns into a lack of self-care, which has at points depleted me and left me with nothing to give.

Making a new concerted effort to give to myself instead has allowed me to say to the universe and everyone around me that I am no longer just going to take whatever I am handed (or not handed). I have the power to create something different and give to myself.

Taking care of my needs, rather than waiting for someone else to do it for me, has gotten me out of the mind-set of scarcity, which not only discouraged me, but prevented me from receiving help from others. To give to Zoey, I have to be full first. Actively making sure that I'm consistently filling up my tank is hard work, but it's game changing when there's no one else around to hold you.

The more I've invested in my emotional and physical health, the more energy I have to be present for Zoey and to enjoy our time together. We've started cooking and playing together more. I come back from my retreats and meditation really, really wanting to be there with her. I've found myself being kinder to her rather than snapping when she, like every other child, doesn't put her shoes on fast enough or something trivial like that. By caring for myself, I've created more room in my heart to recognize opportunities for us to connect with each other.

My Spiritual Master encourages us to avoid investing in the Band-Aids as we raise our children. In the end, we're here to support them, but we also don't have an obligation to go overboard. Children are happy with very little. The desires that we have as adults really stem from our own upbringing, but as parents, we have the power to turn things around and teach our children something different. We're all taught to want what we want but acquiring "things" is not what really makes a difference at a deeper level.

This lesson reassures me and gives me permission to further budget both my money and time. What am I placing value on? What am I creating? What am I teaching my daughter by investing time and money this way? These questions guide my thinking.

As I've watched my actions and decisions more closely in this area, I've started seeing how Zoey (and every other child) is surrounded by distractions. In the eyes of this society, I'm a good parent if I provide access to those distractions. That means taking the time and energy to produce money instead of taking those resources and using them to support my daughter emotionally and spiritually.

I firmly believe most toys are detrimental to our children's creativity, training them instead to buy into a material system that values the wrong things. Consequently, I've had to unlearn an artificial standard of what parents are truly expected to give to their children. However, I can choose to live very simply and increase Zoey's and my happiness by finding balance, keeping in mind that both depravation and excess are equally detrimental. I realize that Zoey may resist a life that doesn't look like her friends', but as a parent, my responsibility is to walk in the light and truth as much as my awareness allows. I don't need to let society dictate what my responsibilities are. And, I can model for my daughter that it's okay to be different as long as she's true to herself and her beliefs.

It pains me to see that I once believed Zoey wouldn't be happy without many toys and distractions. But as I've incorporated self-care intentionality into my life, I've become committed to bringing love and care to the forefront, prioritizing them as basic needs over and above toys, candy, and entertainment. To truly care for my daughter means to do my part to not condition her to get caught up in that material world. What's more valuable is the guidance and tools I can provide to help her embrace her own spiritual mind-set, and to be compassionate and loving with everyone she meets. Though I have practices that have helped me, I always let her know that if she chooses a different spiritual path, I will still be there to support her. She doesn't have to believe what I believe. In fact, I would much rather her have her own first-hand experience.

Chapter Nine

A S I'VE DISPELLED THE drama, cleared my plate of tasks that do not support our new life, and set a higher standard for our lifestyle, I have become more proactive and now welcome each new day. To get here, I've had to become more efficient and skilled at tackling the root causes of problems with consciousness and love. For the first time ever, I have time and space for myself and to contemplate. When Zoey goes to bed every night, I have only a few things left to do because I'm no longer procrastinating. I take out my "acts of devotion" list, otherwise known as my to-do-list, and identify the next most urgent task.

Many nights, the exhaustion creeps in. I look at myself in the mirror with an I'm-ready-to-give-up look in my eyes. Instead of succumbing to that thought, I put some lipstick on, even if I'm already wearing my pajamas, and dance as I do the dishes. I also want to take advantage of every minute I have to keep moving forward spiritually, so I listen to talks from my Spiritual Master as I fold laundry. Other nights, I need to honor my true need to rest and I kick back with a good TV show.

When I'm done taking care of my tasks for the night, I sit in my living room, surrounded by candles, dimmed lights, music, and a good book. I don't always read the book fully. Sometimes, I sit there, contemplating the last sentence I read or just closing my eyes as I leave the day behind.

The more time I spend building a purposeful life in which every need, whether material or spiritual, is fulfilled with love and devotion, the harder it becomes to go back to work the next day. I have loved my career and invested years in it. But now that I have clarity about what I need and what excess looks like in my own life, I see greed all around me. The contrast between the life I've created and my career becomes hard to reconcile. At work, everyone wants more money, to be right, to be the one with the best idea. At home, I'm letting go of control and exploring what really supports me and Zoey.

I still remember when all those false illusions of success were my motivation to keep climbing further and further up the corporate ladder. I used to be willing to do anything to be recognized at work. Now, all I want is to have free time to be with Zoey, enjoy my candle-lit book readings, or meditate on how to become freer from all the expectations I put on myself. The more I think about my current career in marketing, the more I wish I could occupy my days in a way that doesn't involve making someone else more money.

I recognize we're somehow brainwashed into going through the checklist, creating a life that feels à la carte, but in reality, the set items on the menu offer so many potential combinations. We all need a job. We all need to pay a mortgage. We all need to take our kids to school. It becomes easy to measure success by how much money we make or even how successful or intelligent our children are. I don't want to measure success that way anymore.

Today, I see this setup of assigning value to ourselves through the evidence of material success as a drug. Being praised may have initially prevented me from getting depressed; it was even exciting and exhilarating at times. But if someone didn't like something I had done the next day, the validation would go down the drain, and the pain would come back. In that instant, I would lose all sense of purpose and worth, completely altering my mood. But I started seeing these two sides of the coin— when I was in my high and in my low. I was completely dependent on validation from something outside myself and under the mighty power of that drug.

I've since detached my sense of worth from my work. With that, a desire to tap into a bigger purpose, something that I cared about, has awakened within me. I want an environment where my actions have a real impact on someone's life. And for the first time since leaving my marriage and starting a new life, I feel I have the time and space to contemplate what I am really meant to do on this planet.

I know I wasn't meant to just keep my head above water and manage drama. That much is clear. I'm not here to make other people money either. I am meant to create something more meaningful in my life and feel inspired by the opportunity to explore what that might be. I've always felt that there is some way I need to contribute. Finding out what that might be is my new focus.

I've had professionals read my natal chart and akashic records to learn about my gifts and what might be holding me back. While insightful, that hasn't answered my deepest questions about my existence. I keep feeling like there is something I need to do, so I've decided to go on another retreat to see if I can access more information about my destiny.

As I sit down to meditate, I don't ask for less chaos or for God to show me the way out of a painful situation. I want to be shown something I can't yet see about my bigger contribution to this world. Now that I'm not buried in as much unnecessary suffering, I have space to ask myself deeper questions and perhaps make a bigger impact.

I clear my mind and surrender to the moment, letting God show me what can be discovered without me imposing my own agenda. I get pulled into my heart and deeper into my chest, where I now know so much magic dwells. Unlike years ago, when I first started meditating, I'm not afraid of what I'll find when I close my eyes and start the journey within.

As I relax, I follow a breathing pattern meant to move stuck energy. As I focus my attention on breathing in and out, there isn't room for my mind. I feel a tightness around my heart. It feels like the deepest sadness. I place my awareness on my chest and all around my heart and breathe into it.

What happens next is hard to explain, but it has an undeniable emotional impact on me. I'm presented with a vision of a young little girl, probably about five years old, dead, face-down in a ditch. I can't see her face but know I have a deep connection with her, because I immediately feel an intense pain. As I explore the scene, I find a shadow of myself on my knees and next to the ditch sobbing. The pain feels like experiencing my own death, I imagine, and seeing my daughter dying all at once. In that moment, it all feels incredibly real. I can only stay there for a few minutes; it feels like the depth of this sadness may consume me completely.

As I bring my awareness back to the meditation room, I feel my body in a kneeling position, just like the shadow next to the ditch. I hear a whisper as the scene fades away, "Start with Zoey." I don't know where this voice is coming from—God? My Higher Self? But I know it's wiser than me and that I should listen.

As I let this sink in for the next few minutes, there's a knowledge that I have to start where I am. There is something I still have to learn from my current situation. Whatever my purpose is on this journey or what my soul needs to experience, it starts right now, caring for Zoey. And that's all I need to know.

Then, I feel this motherly instinct take over me out of nowhere. All this time, I have been pushing it down because it was just too painful to care that much, but I still recognize what this is. For the past few years, I have actively rejected this motherly love because I believed it made me vulnerable and weak when I needed to be strong. I have been holding onto a belief that I can't be strong as well as vulnerable, sweet, and soft. I chose to be serious and vigilant like a soldier. I thought I couldn't take care when I had to take charge.

I hear it clearly now, and then I feel it in my body. I give it permission by saying out loud, "Let this motherly love flow through my veins." It feels strong—not forced, but unshakeable. There is nothing weak about it. It doesn't take long for me to stand up and start dancing. I put my hands up in the air. Each finger tries to touch the sky, one at a time. I lose myself as I tap into my feminine energy and flow. I feel the infinite love in my heart. I feel free.

Can I be feminine and strong at the same time? Can I wrap my arms around my daughter in absolute love and tenderness, and still protect her from anything in this world? Can I do that for myself? Can I take this motherly instinct and give myself that hug I have always longed for?

I grew up with a mother who was incredibly strong. She took charge in our home and made sure we all had dinner on the table every night. I have four siblings, and a father whose strength is being creative and making everyone laugh. But she had to make sure we were all organized, and without her, our lives would have been incredibly chaotic.

She wanted to protect us, feed us, and make sure we were healthy and surrounded by the right people. As a child, that's what I learned, and that's the woman I became. But as I grew up, I lost my connection to another part of myself. There was a softness, a sensitivity missing. I became a thinker, someone who could solve problems logically and didn't think she needed all that touchy-feely stuff. When I saw others cry for no reason or have emotional reactions that didn't let them think clearly, I saw them as weak.

But right now, right here, I am encouraged by a crack of light showing me that both perhaps can live together—that both feelings and thinking can coexist.

I wonder how this new perspective will impact my daughter.

Should I perhaps stop asking Zoey to just feel her feelings and be strong, and instead hold space for her to curl up and cry in my arms?

It isn't that I don't allow her to feel her feelings. I feel mine, too. But somehow I have created a concept in my mind that all of that is private business, something we should individually deal with. I show her my love, but I don't ever break down and show her the true, soft side of me. How will she ever feel she has permission to be vulnerable and fall apart when all I model is strength?

All of a sudden, the reason why she asked me not long ago, why I never cried, becomes clear. I never let myself cry in front of her. I put on a mask. I cry on my own behind closed doors and then only show her the aftermath—me victoriously walking out, ready to take on the world. Has this set an unrealistic expectation of what strength looks like? Am I inadvertently modeling the false idea that there are shortcuts to true empowerment? I have experienced, and want to teach her, that the only way is to face everything that wants to break us down.

Though I entered this retreat hoping to find some greater purpose, all I needed to learn was simply that being a mom was the way to an open heart. It turns out my extraordinary purpose has been right in front of me this whole time. I can learn what I need to learn and give what I need to contribute where I already am.

I've since become truly connected with my destiny as a mother and started appreciating what it takes to guide another soul. Zoey has her own path, just like I have mine. Lucky for both of us, we are walking at least this part together. I realize I have no control over what's going to happen to her, and it fills me with a compassion that I have never had before. I'm falling in love with the motherly side of me that I hid away before. I realize now how hard I've been on Zoey, always urging her to push forward in spite of it all. How unfair. Why couldn't I just honor her own process?

I've started seeing Zoey in a new light, or maybe I've finally given myself permission to fully feel how I've always felt for her. We've always been great buddies. We've always had more of a peer-to-peer relationship without a forced hierarchy or imposed authority (I call her my little human-in-training). I respect both what her soul is experiencing now, as well as where it will go. It just so happens my soul is in her mother's body this time around. And, if I'm being honest, with as wise as she can be, I wouldn't be surprised if her soul had been my soul's mother in a previous lifetime.

Being a mom is a huge part of who I am today. Without that experience, I wouldn't have learned all these critical lessons. I also wouldn't have opened my heart in the way that I have. Embracing this fact has changed my whole perspective. I'm no longer looking for relief from her, like I used to. Zoey is a wonderful child, and I am incredibly grateful to be part of her journey. I've realized there isn't a bigger purpose I need to be looking for. Things will reveal themselves, and right now, what is in front of me is a beautiful opportunity for me to grow as I guide and support this other soul.

Chapter Ten

M Y FAILED ATTEMPTS AT dating in the couple of years after my divorce have taught me that the way human relationships work, especially romantic ones, is unfair and exhausting to everyone involved. We pull on each other. We expect everything from each other. We expect each other to fix our inherent unworthiness. We put so much pressure on the other to make ourselves happy and provide exactly what we need. And when we don't get it, we get triggered and push each other away.

I recognize this pattern even with Zoey, when she wants love and I want space. As I let go of more and more of my own expectations of her, I've learned that I can't always give her what she wants. I also have no ownership of her, and she doesn't owe me anything either.

This realization has impacted how I view all relationships. All we can do is choose to continue to walk the path together, to have compassion for each other, to know that we're all doing our best with what we know and what we have to give.

The more I learn about unconditional love and my own blocks and triggers, the more I convince myself that it is pretty much impossible for me to find someone who sees the world the same as me. For a while, I even look for opportunities to prove to myself that such a man doesn't exist. But in a last-ditch effort to prove it is going to be hard for me to find that kind of partner, I connect with someone who I would have completely judged and dismissed in the past. He doesn't fit my type, if you will. But he introduces himself by asking for my thoughts on some of the deepest questions I had been pondering for years.

Ben and I met at a tiny art gallery in the very small town where I live. As I walked up the steps, I saw his smile and then his eyes, and I just knew there was something special about him. Even though I didn't want to admit it, we connected immediately. I had never felt so safe in someone's presence before. I'd learned to take care of myself, but I knew I wanted to see him again about an hour into our twelve-hour-long first date.

Soon enough, Ben moved in after meeting and gaining Zoey's approval. He was not a dad, and going into this relationship, we both knew adding the element of co-parenting would be a learning experience for us. He had been single for a very long time and had his own space, which he had happily embraced. For my part, I had to let go of my concern that my love for Zoey and Ben individually wouldn't be enough to bring the three of us together, and that they may never learn to love each other.

Luckily, Ben proved to be incredibly sweet with Zoey. He cooks us delicious dinners every night and is a natural protector. He grew up without a father, so he can empathize with Zoey's sense of loss. Having been brought up by a single mother himself, he seems to have a natural sense for how to support me. He makes us laugh when we both need it most, and he's engaging when reading us bedtime stories, changing his voice to fit each of the characters.

Perhaps unavoidably, as we've gotten to know each other and started sharing a routine and space, we've all found ways we trigger each other. Not long after moving in, Ben started expressing that there was a lack of boundaries. He would come home exhausted from work and need space and silence. His desire not to talk to anyone or interact was absolutely puzzling to Zoey and me, as we're both extroverts who crave connection. We immediately felt rejected.

Other things also came up. Ben would get upset with Zoey when she tried to get away with something or played victim. He didn't like when she had a tantrum right after coming back from seeing her dad. Whenever I explained what Zoey had been through and what the motivations behind her behavior might be, Ben felt I was justifying her actions, and the arguments quickly became heated. I explained how she's a human in training and that her soul has gone through so much. His response has been an explanation of how different his childhood had been. We went into long conversations about triggers and how our feelings are never someone else's fault, but our reactions to our own sense of unworthiness.

And, then, I took a moment to ask myself different questions. Why was I trying so hard to defend my parenting philosophy? What was I triggered by? When, in my mind, Ben rejected Zoey, I felt he was rejecting me. In reality, he wasn't doing either, but my own trauma of having felt abandoned and rejected in my marriage was now carrying over into my new relationship. Along the journey, I had created a concept that no man would ever love both Zoey and me enough to want to be in our life.

Understanding my own motivations has deepened my relationship with Ben. He's helped me identify the flaws in the parenting style I've grown accustomed to. Today, I'm grateful that I have a partner by my side, showing me a different perspective.

In turn, I've shown him how I identify my own triggers and where they come from. Now that we know each other so well, we can tell when we're about to get into an argument just because we both need something we're not getting. We can now better manage our own triggers, take responsibility, walk away, and feel our feelings first, helping us avoid unnecessarily pushing each other away.

While our relationship hasn't been perfect, this turn of events has been a relief for me. I'm trying to raise Zoey to be aware of her triggers, take responsibility for her own feelings, and know it's best to wait to engage others after intense emotions have passed.

This is how the closest to unconditional love that humans can achieve is possible... when we each assume that every individual has trauma, pain, and triggers; when we have compassion for what the other has been through and try to understand first; when we choose what's best for all, even if it means we don't each get exactly what we want.

This is the kind of relationship that makes it possible to walk our individual paths side by side—not judging but holding each other. If we simply agree to be each other's co-pilot and look into the mirror to find our blind spots, we each take responsibility and avoid a crash.

Going deep into myself has taught me that our default is to let our conditioning, trauma, bad experiences, and insecurities destroy us and everything around us. It takes a tremendous amount of courage and persistence to choose to love every day and observe how I'm engaging in every situation. Am I in the light or in the darkness?

By recognizing that my insecurities and triggers come from within myself, rather than in what Ben and Zoey are "doing wrong," I have a better chance of taking responsibility for my part and finding a loving response. As soon as Ben and I started unpacking what was really happening inside ourselves and how we were filtering each situation through our own pain, a path forward became clear.

The perfect relationship doesn't exist, but it's possible to respect others for who they are, have compassion for what we have all been through, and understand that our reactions and our actions are a result of all of that. Can we change direction? Of course. Every time we make a decision from a place of love, we're supporting each other in our healing, and that is all that matters in the end.

Ben's and my relationship is simply a partnership in which we've decided to be really good friends for each other. We know obstacles will appear, but also that we're going to hold each other through all of it. At the end of the day, we all have blind spots, but when we love someone enough to have compassion for what they're going through, to understand that it's hard to overcome our own weaknesses and faults, then we can be patient. Because we believe in each other, and because we believe that we can actually change the course, we can learn and move forward.

That's what plays out in every relationship. It applies to our children and to all of humanity. Each of us, even if it doesn't look like it, are on a path forward. Sometimes what looks like a setback on the surface is actually the perfect opportunity for us to pause and take a look at what's happening inside ourselves. Only then can we see how we can let go of what's holding us back. Many times, the material circumstances don't need to change. By choosing to engage internally in a different way, the entire outcome can change.

I know from my own experience how hard it is to face oneself, but at this point, I can't even picture being in a relationship with someone who's not up for constant growth and evolution. Even though I don't always recognize Ben for his humility, I know that's what it takes to reflect on a relationship and try to change course. For us, it takes trusting that our love is worth the fight with our own darkness.

Chapter Eleven

SO HERE I AM, back at the beginning. Zoey is finally asleep in bed. Ben and I are recapping the day as I unpack from my interrupted business trip. Our life is about to change. We don't know how long Sean will be in jail this time, but we do know Zoey will likely be with us full time moving forward.

I get another call from an unknown number. I answer, knowing it is likely news about Sean. Even though we have complete choice as to how and whether we'll engage in this new chapter of his life, I still want to understand the situation so that I can support Zoey.

"I don't have a lot of time. I need you to bail me out tonight, please. I can give you the number you need to call."

In my compassion for what he might be going through and my desire for him to be safe, I treat his request as if it was coming from a dear friend. I ask him for more information and tell him I need to look into it. I have no idea what it will take. As I hang up, I wonder why I'm still the one he calls for help. How is that still my role in his life? But exploring that thought is not worth my time.

After making a few phone calls, I find it would take thousands of dollars and becoming legally accountable for his actions for me to help him get out right now. I can't do that financially, and I can't take the risk that something might go wrong. I call Sean's dad to update him and see if he is willing to take on Sean's request.

"He called me first," Sean's dad tells me as his voice breaks. "I am done enabling him. He will need to find his own way out this time."

I don't think any parent wants to give up on their child, but part of letting them walk their path is letting them fall on their face if that's what they need to go through next. I have new respect for Sean's father. I hate the idea of not supporting Sean, or anyone for that matter, but I know in my gut his father is right. We each have to fight our own demons, and no one else can do it for us.

"Don't do it, Sophie. He needs to get himself out of this one."

I'm grateful that Sean's dad and I still have this trusting, caring relationship. I listen and agree.

There is still a part of me that feels guilty, but I also know this is the right thing to do. Just as I was tempted to follow that initial instinct to help him (society says you should always help a friend), I know deep down bailing out Sean is not the help he needs. When I'm centered in my heart and the external pressure of what I should do falls away, I want everyone to find true freedom. I can't play God by interfering in what anyone needs to go through. If I derail Sean's current course, he may never learn the lesson he needs to learn. I instead pray he finds what he needs to propel his own life forward.

As I hang up the phone, I open my bedroom door to find Zoey on the other side.

"Did you hear Mommy on the phone?" I ask as I kneel down to hold her.

"Yes, I heard everything. You and Grandpa don't want to help Daddy get out of jail."

"Do you know why?"

"He needs to deal with the consequences. I understand."

I have never kept anything from her. I have always been honest without criticizing her dad, giving the facts each time he has stumbled.

"If you do something against the rules, and Mommy grounds you so you have time to think about it, is it fair for me to give you a way out?"

"No. When I do something against the rules, I have to learn."

Zoey's maturity always astounds me. She understands complex dynamics, processes what's happening, and can communicate her wise conclusion clearly each time. This is the upside of the pain she's gone through.

I explain to her that both her grandfather and I want the best for her dad, and this time he has to figure things out on his own. She says she understands and gives me a big hug. I walk her back to bed and kiss her goodnight once again. I'm proud that she's not afraid to talk about what she's experiencing. I'm proud of her for learning from the experience. I hope one day this will serve her in some way.

The next day, as I kiss Zoey good morning and prepare her

breakfast, I know without doubt I was meant to be her mother. She truly is one of the greatest gifts in my life, and I don't say that just because she happens to be my daughter. I say that because she has shown me things I would have never been able to see on my own. Zoey challenges me to love myself, to see when I'm not acting from a place of love. She cares so deeply about everyone. She's creative and unafraid of being herself. She's the child who stops to give a stranger a compliment and even asks bullies whether they have pain in their heart and need a friend. She believes no one should be left behind.

My gratitude for this experience I've had continues to grow. Even after going to sleep crying or running to Zoey countless times, everything that has happened has allowed me to grow and face something new in myself. Today, I love like I never thought I could love before—not just others, but also myself. I truly appreciate how far I've come.

I've learned to have more compassion, even when things are not going my way. No matter the impulse in me, I care more for my ex-husband today than I did through all the years when he was in and out of rehab and jail, or when he wasn't there for my daughter. When I think of what he's endured, I can only hope that he finds his way out of his suffering.

No, it hasn't been easy for me. I've had to take care of my daughter in every single way. That's just simply what's best for her, and he can't be there for her now. I've forgiven him.

Also, I have finally found compassion for myself. I've had to learn my own lessons and choose to take the high road, even when I just wanted to take a break. But I've done it, and I've done it with love. I think if nothing else, this experience has opened my heart in a way I never thought possible.

I've also learned to have compassion for my daughter,

which helps me see her predicament. We each have our own struggles in this world. I now understand that, try as I may, I'm not fully responsible for the outcome of her life or for how she navigates it. There's no guarantee that she won't be hurt—in fact, the default is she will be. She still needs to discover who she is, where she wants to go, and how. While I did choose her father, there's a bigger plan in their relationship that is beyond my control. What I can take responsibility for, however, is the safety I provide for her. In addition, I can use everything I've learned on my journey to guide her through her own pain. But, that's just the icing on the cake.

The truth that's beyond my understanding, but I still hold in my heart as a compass for every decision, is that she's on this earth to walk her own path.

Chapter Twelve

AS I'M KISSING ZOEY goodnight under her canopy, she asks me to sit on her bed. She has something she wants to talk to me about. Her best friend sometimes wants to play with other girls who don't like Zoey, and that makes her feel sad.

"I understand how you feel. There are people who don't like me, too. It makes me sad, but it's true. Do you have friends who love you?"

"Yes," she says, lighting up. Then she looks down and gets serious. "I like writing in my diary at night when I feel sad about those other girls not liking me."

"That's good! That's why I meditate. I need to shake my feelings out too. Then, I can find more love for myself, the people who want to be my friends, and those who don't."

"Thank you, Mom. You're trustworthy and my best friend. I love you."

"Thank you for sharing how you're feeling with me, Monkey. I love and trust you, too."

As I turn the light off and walk out of her room, I take a deep breath and reflect. Today was just another perfectly imperfect day. I'm pretty sure I yelled at Zoey this morning when I woke up with a splitting headache. I will apologize tomorrow; that was uncalled for. Zoey and I also had a tea party in the afternoon. It was fun to talk to her and hear all about the new song she's writing. She wants to be a pop star. And, most importantly, she trusts me and wants to share what's going on inside her with me. Even with the ups and downs, my heart is full.

That's how a lot of days go. I have to balance what's happening with me, whether it's work or a cold, with what Zoey needs. It would be ridiculous for me to even imply that I'm the living example of everything I've learned along this journey every single day. The impostor syndrome and doubt about whether I'm doing any of this right will always be there. As humans, it's our nature to feel inadequate, have moments of weakness, and feel unworthy. Still, all these lessons are stored in my heart and guide me, even when my conditioning and learned behaviors try to pull me in a different direction.

Half the battle is making a choice every day to stay in the light, steering myself toward the love and light, and trusting God's got me. I also trust that the truth is within me and that I can always find it, if I'm willing to let go of the excuses, avoid denial, and be brutally honest about what's really happening inside. I'm not going to claim it's easy, because it's not. It takes extreme honesty with myself. Only from that place can I see the truth. Only from that place can I make a choice about trying something new. Only from that place can I see when I'm blaming and making up excuses not to take responsibility.

All those years, I made life more difficult than it needed

to be. But I didn't like seeing myself as a victim. I never liked how money and guilt got in the way of supporting my daughter and myself. There were hard moments where I could see the darkness of the decisions I was making, and those feelings needed to be felt. I made an intentional decision to change direction, and it took trial and error. Making any type of change requires being willing to face ourselves and accept that adjusting to change is often a lifelong journey.

I have learned that feelings are the doorway into connection, into better decision-making, into a consciousness of being an observer. From this place, I can discern what I'm trying to do just because I'm tired, resentful, exhausted, mad, angry, or wishing things were different.

My heart has broken for everyone, all of us in this world, including myself. We all go through pain, find the light, and get sucked into the darkness without fair warning every day. The part I need to be responsible for is how I engage with what is and whether I feel and act from a place of love in my heart. I've learned about trust and attachments. When I don't listen, it's because I don't want to let go of something. That, I've learned, is how I protect myself. But I want to be an example of what love looks like every day—in the way I drive, in how I respect people in grocery stores, in how I smile at the homeless on the street. Then I can get my ego out of the way.

My Spiritual Master encourages us to ask ourselves, "How can you live so you are conscious your entire life and hold the highest level of care, devotion, and love within yourself?"

The first time I heard this question, the task felt impossible. How could I, a simple mortal, ever do that? But since I first heard this question, I've realized all she's asking is for me to aim for moment-by-moment awareness. No one expects me to achieve this overnight. Taking that ultimate goal and setting a deadline to achieve this state is completely unrealistic. The objective is a lot simpler: to become freer and freer every day, slowly, patiently, knowing that there will be setbacks, knowing that I won't always make the right choice or have enough awareness, because I'm human.

Whoever has visited me knows my home can sometimes get messy. I just do my best to keep up with everything that needs to be done, get help when needed, and try to make it as beautiful as possible. Whoever has talked to me after work knows that I sometimes get triggered and rant about something, even if my intention is to bring my best self to work and be patient and compassionate with everyone. I sometimes snap at Zoey, and then I realize I haven't been taking proper care of myself.

I sometimes feel rejected by Ben and get emotional. Eventually, I'm able to see how my trauma may have gotten to me, and I'll meditate in search of that unwavering self-love that can help me forgive or understand where he may be internally.

Transformation doesn't happen overnight, but over time, through each conscious choice to go within for answers born of love and truth. From here come small successes, little shifts toward love instead of separation that make a difference in the long run. And the best part is, I don't have to do it all on my own. In every meditation and reflection, God is ready to hold and guide me.

There's a magic that happens in meditation that is intangible but real. Every shift is here to stay, even when a temporary setback is enough evidence for my mind to convince me otherwise. Each decision to be vulnerable enough to just wonder where I have gotten caught up in my own pain, exhaustion, drama and trauma has long-term effects.

"How can you live so you are conscious your entire life and hold the highest level of care, devotion, and love within yourself?"

I once thought that was such a big question because I immediately put pressure on myself to just do it. I took it on like any other project and started driving toward the finish line. But since learning how to go within, I've also learned how to tap into a truth that can't be found in my mind. It's the truth of what's left once everything that is born of my human ways— reaction, triggers, and feelings— have been shaken off. It's that bare truth that shows me the way. Believer or not, if you've ever looked up at the sky and said a prayer, not one of those that you memorize, but those that just flow from your heart, then you have hope that someone is listening.

You don't have to believe in a higher being or that the universe has a mind of its own. But if nothing else, believe that you have a higher self. We're all more powerful than we realize, and we can make all of this happen for ourselves.

My Spiritual Master says that we will all feel that longing at some point. Underneath all the emotions and feelings and thoughts, there's that empty space inside ourselves. No matter what we do, no matter what material satisfaction or shelter we seek, eventually it all fades away. We've tried it all. Eating, relationships, successful careers. Nothing quite does it. And as we go deeper into this longing, the pain becomes more intense, yet it has a very different taste. It sometimes feels like falling into the abyss, and we don't know who will catch us.

As I've gone through my divorce and everything that's happened after, I have often wondered who would hold me. I am grateful that I found a path that would help me see. As I reflect upon my story, I sometimes trick myself and think I haven't really done anything extraordinary. I didn't spend months in India searching for enlightenment. I haven't changed my life externally, completely. Everything—every single change—happened within.

Today, even in an amazing relationship, knowing that I have found the man I'm going to spend the rest of my life with, I still know it's not his responsibility to hold me. I have learned that nothing—literally nothing—existing outside myself can fix the emptiness. In the end, when the lights are off, when I'm exhausted and have completed all my chores, the only one who will hold me is me. And when I say me, I mean that part of me that belongs to Spirit, that part that belongs to God.

BECAUSE EVERY SINGLE MOTHER HAS A STORY...

I'd love to hear yours.

THE AWAKENING SINGLE MOM

is a community where single mothers can get up-close and personal with the material from the book "Who Will Hold Me? A Single Mother's Memoir of Self-Love, Empowerment & Freedom." It's a drama-free, blame-free space for all single moms embarking on their own journey of self-discovery and seeking support in a shared experience.

Members can enjoy the inside track on specific tools and practices that have helped Sophie and join her on weekly calls answering questions and sharing experiences.

It's also a place where other single moms who are on a similar path can connect with one another and share their own tips and gems they've picked up along the way.

JOIN THE COMMUNITY BY SCANNING THE QR CODE

Made in the USA
Monee, IL
10 April 2020